THE STEP BY STEP ART OF

Silk Painting

CLB 4337
© 1995 CLB Publishing, Godalming, Surrey, England
Printed and bound in Singapore by Tien Wah Press
All rights reserved
ISBN 1-85833-419-5

THE STEP BY STEP ART OF

Silk Painting

Text and Designs by
JAN EATON
Photography by
STEVE TANNER

COOMBE BOOKS

Contents

Equipment

Silk painting is a fascinating hobby offering scope for experimenting with different types of silk decorated with exotic colour and pattern combinations. Each project in the book specifies which fabric and colour combination were used to make the item in the photograph, but feel free to experiment, keeping in mind the information given in the techniques section overleaf. All the designs have been created using colours which are easily made colour-fast using a domestic iron.

Silk Paints

There are several brands of iron-fix paint to choose from, each one offering a slightly different palette of colours, and various brands can be used side by side on the same piece of work. To try out the effect of various colours before embarking on a piece of work, make up a colour sample as shown on page 15. When working, take care to keep each bottle of paint clean by transferring the paint to a palette with an eye dropper before starting to paint. Apply silk paints to the silk using a paintbrush, cotton bud or eye dropper, depending on the technique used.

Outliner

Liquid paints move and flow when applied to fabric due to capillary action. To control this movement, a material called a resist is used which, when applied to the fabric in continuous lines and allowed to dry, separates and confines the paint to pre-determined areas. The resist used in silk painting is called outliner or gutta. Water-based outliner has been used for all the projects in the book – it is easy to handle, especially for a beginner, and does not thicken during warm weather or with age. Outliner is available in clear, gold, silver, copper and several other metallic colours. For beginners, it is useful to remember that mistakes look less noticeable when using a clear outliner.

10

Outliner Bottles

Apply outliner to the fabric using an outliner bottle make from pliable plastic. The simplest type has a plastic nozzle which you cut before use, but the easiest to use has a screw- or push-on metal nib. The nibs are available in a range of sizes, depending on the weight of line required, but the most useful one has a fine nib. After use, wash out the outliner bottle thoroughly with cold water, paying particular attention to the nib. A piece of thin wire is supplied with each nib to help you with the cleaning process.

Frames

Silk frames come in many sizes and most of them adjust easily to cope with a range of fabric squares and rectangles. When painting a scarf, you will need to use the largest frame available, while many of the smaller projects can be painted using a small sample frame about 30cm (12in) square. Take the time to protect the top surface of your frame with strips of masking tape before pinning the pieces of silk in position. Renew the tape each time you use the frame.

Silk pins and Map tacks

Three-point silk pins have three slim points and are specially designed to hold fabric securely in a frame without damaging the weave. Never use drawing pins, as the thick point will split the fabric threads and cause unsightly holes. When painting a ready-made scarf, use map tacks instead of 3-point silk pins, inserting the tacks through the rolled hem of the scarf.

Brushes, Foam brushes and Cotton buds

Brushes for silk painting are available in a huge range of sizes and materials, from Chinese brushes with long natural bristles to artist's brushes containing synthetic fibres. In general, brushes with long bristles work best for painting silk as the long bristles hold large amounts of paint, but the final choice is very much a matter of personal preference. You will need to buy several sizes of paintbrush, from a tiny one for colouring small, intricate details to large wash brush for painting backgrounds. A foam brush consists of a flat strip of sturdy foam fastened to a wooden handle. Available in several sizes, foam brushes are useful for painting large areas very quickly. Cotton buds provide a useful alternative to brushes – they have the advantage of being cheap to buy and can be thrown away after use, but are less successful when negotiating intricate details.

Palettes and Eye droppers

Buy a white china or plastic palette with large divisions and several eye droppers. Transfer each colour of paint to the palette using a separate dropper for each colour. Eye droppers made of glass are available from a chemist's shop.

Fade-away Embroidery Marker

The marker is filled with a special ink which fades when exposed to the air. Fading time will vary due to atmospheric conditions, but the maximum time the drawn design will remain visible on the fabric is about 72 hours.

Salt

Try using different types of salt for the dry salt technique – they will give varying results due to the different crystal sizes. Effect salt is available from specialist textile shops, but also try sea salt, dishwasher salt and rock salt. Use either table or cooking salt to make a salt solution as they dissolve easily. Keep salt in an airtight container to prevent it from attracting moisture.

Wax

Use batik wax for the wax crackle technique. Batik wax is a mixture of several types of wax and is formulated to give good crisp creases and crackles.

Polythene Sheet

Useful for keeping work surfaces clean when painting and vital for the scrunch painting technique, thin polythene sheets are available in several sizes from builder's merchants.

Materials

Types of Silk

Silk comes in various weights and different weaves. Irregularities in the weave, particularly in the heavier fabrics such as dupion and Thai silk, are part of the nature of the material and should not be considered as flaws. For silk painting-using the outliner technique, fabrics with a smooth surface such as Habotai silk work best, while salt techniques and scrunch painting will be successful on most types. The swatches on the left show a number of different silk types, but there are many more available in the shops. You can buy specially prepared white and off-white silk from specialist textile shops. This silk has been degummed and has no chemical dressing which means it will not need washing. When using coloured or unprepared silk, wash, dry and press it before painting to remove any chemical residue. Use a mild soap such as baby shampoo to wash silk and add a dash of white vinegar to the final rinse.

Habotai

A smooth, evenly woven silk also known as Chinese or Japanese silk, Habotai is available in a number of weights. The thinnest Habotai, 5, is excellent for making scarves and handkerchiefs and has a fine, gauzy appearance. The medium weight, 8, is a good, all-purpose fabric especially suited to the outliner and wax crackle techniques. Washed silk is heavy weight Habotai which has been pre-washed to create a thick, slippery fabric which is excellent for stencilling and scrunch painting.

Twill

Slightly patterned with a pronounced diagonal weave, twill silk is slightly heavier than Habotai silk and works well with the outliner technique. The weave has a tendency to spread colour in a specific direction, so apply the outliner in a heavy line and check that there are no breaks.

Sheer Silks

Chiffon and georgette are fine, semi-transparent silks used mainly for scarves. Most techniques work well with these fabrics, with the exception of wax crackle.

Taffeta and Spun Silk

A stiff, rather heavy silk with a dense weave, taffeta is good for stencilled and sprayed designs. Spun silk is slightly shiny and has a more open weave than taffeta. It is often patterned with woven stripes and checks.

Dupion and Thai

Available in a wide range of colours as well as patterned with woven stripes, checks and ikat designs, dupion is a sturdy silk with irregular slubs running throughout the weave. It is suitable for scrunch painting, dry salt, stencilled and sprayed techniques, but outliner does not penetrate this fabric. Thai silk is similar in appearance, but woven with a finer, more lustrous thread.

Noil

Made from waste silk left over after the better quality fabrics have been made, silk noil looks rather like cotton fabric. The surface is nubby and uneven, with a very slight sheen, but it takes stencilled designs well.

Fancy Silks

This term includes fabric with woven patterns and textures, as well as those incorporating metallic threads. The most readily available is Jacquard silk which has a woven relief design that picks up and reflects light.

Crêpe De Chine

Crêpe de chine is a matt silk with a velvety feel. It drapes well and is excellent for making scarves and garments. Paint flows unevenly on crêpe de chine so it is very difficult to paint an area of smooth, flat colour, but scrunch painting works exceptionally well with this fabric.

A single drop of silk paint was applied to each of these samples.

SILK CHIFFON
On silk chiffon, the drop spreads over small area and it dries quickly, leaving a very dark edge round the shape. The outliner technique works well with this fabric.

SPUN SILK
Spun silk takes the colour well, although the single drop of paint spreads over a limited area due to the weight of the yarn. This type of silk works well used for sprayed or scrunch painted techniques.

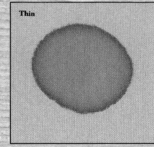

Thin

THIN AND MEDIUM HABOTAI
On thin, 5 Habotai, the paint flows and spreads easily. The effect is similar on medium weight Habotai but the spread is slightly larger. Both these types of silk are perfect for decorating with the outliner technique.

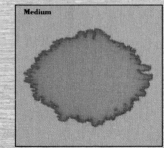

Medium

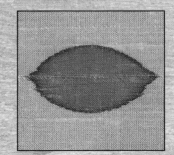

SILK DUPION
Here, the paint flows thickly over the surface. But the outliner technique does not work with this fabric. Heavy silk like this is best used for sprayed and scrunch painted designs.

Techniques

Silk Painting

Always wash, dry and press the fabric to remove any dressing. Prepare the frame by applying strips of masking tape along the edges. This protects the wood and helps avoid paint being transferred to the next piece. Pin fabric to the frame with 3-point silk pins, or map tacks if you are decorating a ready-make scarf. This will minimise fabric damage. Apply the paint with cotton buds or paintbrushes. To gauge the finished colour effect, make a colour chart (bottom right) using Habotai silk. Stretch the silk in a frame and, using clear outliner, make squares for each colour of paint you have. Paint, then allow to dry, and note the number of each paint below the square.

1 Pin the fabric to the frame using 3-point silk pins or map tacks, placing them about 4cm (1½in) apart, making sure that the grain of the fabric is straight. The fabric should be held taut in the frame.

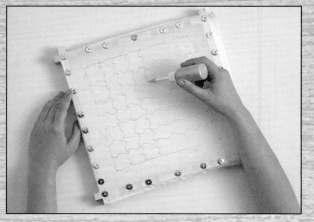

2 Stir the outliner thoroughly and transfer it to the outliner bottle. Squeeze gently over scrap paper until the outliner flows evenly through the nib. Touching the nib to the fabric, apply in a continuous line.

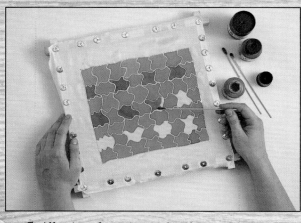

5 Allowing the paint to dry thoroughly between applications, add the remaining colours to the design, discarding and replacing the used cotton bud with a fresh one for each colour. When colouring a large design, work outwards from the centre to avoid smudging.

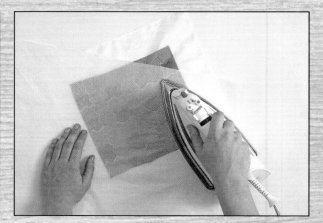

6 Leave the finished painting to dry for about 48 hours, longer if using a metallic outliner. To fix the colours, sandwich the fabric right side down between white tissue paper and press with a hot iron for two minutes. Rinse the fabric in cool water to remove surplus paint, allow to dry, then press lightly on the wrong side with a cool iron.

3 Allow the outliner to dry completely before proceeding – this may take several hours. Stir the silk paint vigorously. Apply the first colour using a cotton bud. Soak the bud in paint, then press it on to the fabric and allow the paint to flood across the outlined shape. Add more paint until the shape is filled.

4 Leave the first colour to dry, then apply the second colour using a fresh cotton bud. You will soon learn how much paint to apply to each shape, but remember that the heavier the coat of paint, the darker the finished result will be. The paint covering large shapes may dry unevenly and require a second coat – make sure that the first coat is dry before adding a second.

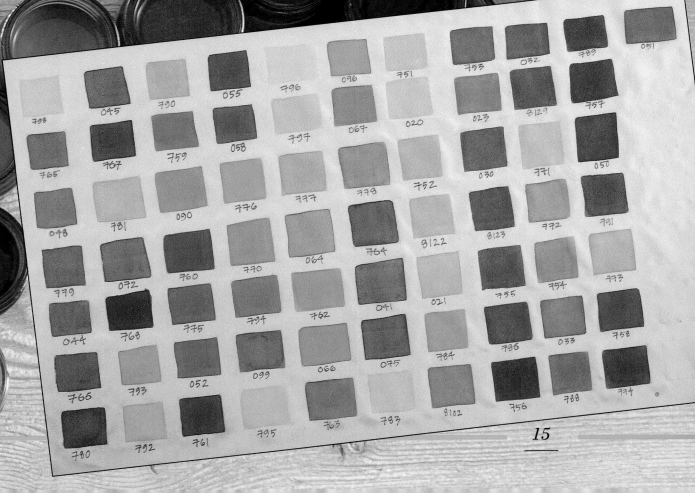

Salt Solution

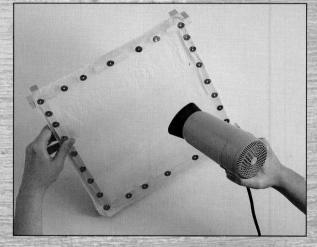

1 Silk soaked in salt solution creates an interesting effect when painted. The painted shapes have an unusual dotted texture with uneven, crystalline edges. Prepare the salt solution by placing 3 tablespoons of cooking salt in a heatproof bowl and adding 500ml of boiling water. Stir with a metal spoon to dissolve the salt and leave the solution to cool.

2 Wash and dry the silk to remove any dressing. Immerse the silk in the cold salt solution, pressing it down with the spoon. Leave to soak for a few minutes, then remove and hang to dry. You can vary the effect by adding more or less salt to alter the strength of the solution, remembering that a stronger solution will give the applied paint a more crystalline appearance.

3 Instead of soaking the silk in a bowl, you can pin the fabric to a silk painting frame with 3-point silk pins and apply the salt solution directly on to the fabric with a large, soft paintbrush. Leave the fabric to dry naturally on the frame, or speed up the drying process by using a hair dryer. After applying and fixing the colours, wash in warm water to remove the salt.

Dry Salt

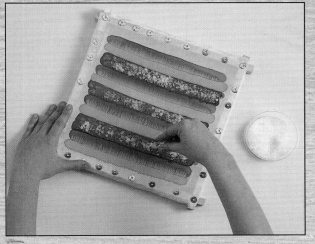

1 Dry salt attracts water, so when it is sprinkled on to wet paint, it creates interesting and unusual effects by soaking up paint. To use this technique, stretch the silk in the frame in the usual way with 3-point silk pins and paint an area of colour with a foam or bristle brush.

2 While the paint is still wet, sprinkle salt across the surface. Different types of salt including sea salt, rock salt and cooking salt give varying results due to the crystal size. You can also achieve different effects by sprinkling salt sparingly or thickly over the silk, or by adding large crystals one by one. Leave to dry, brush off the salt, fix and wash.

3 When combining smoothly painted and salted areas on the same piece of silk, paint the smooth areas first and allow them to dry completely before starting the salted areas. Even a single crystal can spoil a smooth area while paint is still damp, so keep salt safely stored in a screw top jar.

Scrunch Painting

1 *This is the quickest and most immediate method of decorating silk. Begin by washing the silk to remove any dressing, then rinse well in two or three changes of cold, clean water. Wring out the silk gently to remove surplus water. Place a polythene sheet on a flat surface, then lay the wet silk on top. Working with both hands, crumple and scrunch the fabric evenly to create peaks and troughs. Mop up any pools of water from the polythene.*

2 *Using an eye dropper, drop spots of one colour of paint on to the wet silk. Begin with the palest colour and try to spread the spots evenly across the crumpled silk. The paint will quickly spread to form large blotches. Using a separate eye dropper for each colour, repeat this procedure with the remaining colours until the fabric colour is concealed. Allow the silk to dry before lifting it off the polythene – this may take several hours – then fix, and wash to remove surplus dye.*

Wax Crackle

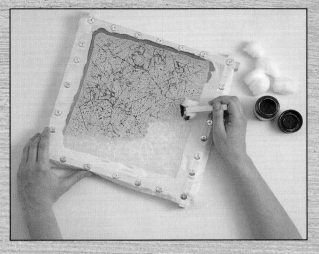

1 *Pin the silk in the frame using 3-point silk pins. Pour some batik wax granules into a heatproof bowl and stand the bowl in an old saucepan containing about 8cm (3in) of simmering water until the wax melts. Leaving the bowl in the pan, spread molten wax evenly across the fabric using an old paintbrush. Top up the water as necessary.*

2 *Carefully remove the waxed silk from the frame. Peel off the masking tape protecting the wood and replace. Place a sheet of newspaper or scrap paper over the work surface and crumple the silk between both hands so that the waxed surface creases and cracks. Crumple the silk lightly for soft crackles, harder for a heavier effect.*

3 *Carefully smooth out the crumpled silk and replace it in the frame. Pour the paint into a saucer or flat container. Holding a cotton wool ball firmly in a spring clothes peg, dip it into the paint and apply to the waxed silk with a circular scrubbing motion. Keep applying paint until the cracks are saturated with colour.*

4 *Leave to dry, then remove the silk from the frame. Place a thick layer of newspaper on a flat surface and cover with clean scrap paper. Place the silk on top and cover with clean paper. Press with a hot iron until the paper is soaked with wax. Change the paper and repeat until all the visible wax has gone. Wash in hot water and detergent to remove any remaining traces of wax.*

Transferring Designs

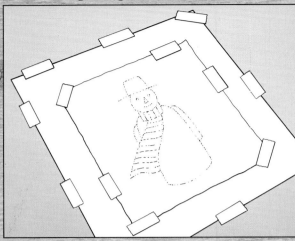

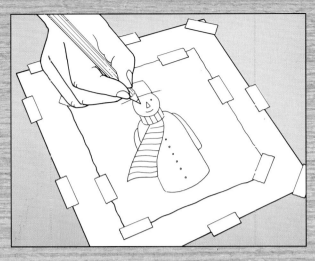

Backing with Interfacing

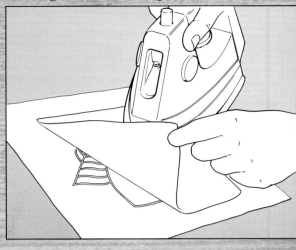

1 To transfer a design to silk before outlining, first wash and press the fabric. Lay the tracing of the design on a flat surface, with right side facing, and secure with strips of masking tape. Lay the silk on top of the tracing and smooth it gently with your hands to remove any wrinkles. Tape in position, making sure that the grain of the silk runs straight and that the design is in the correct position on the fabric. The design shows through the silk quite clearly.

2 Trace the design on the silk using either a soft 2B pencil, or a fade-away embroidery marker. The marker contains special ink which fades when exposed to air, so traced lines will disappear within 72 hours. During damp weather, fading time may be reduced to between 8 and 12 hours.

Back painted silk with iron-on interfacing to give it body. Use a lightweight type for cushions and pelmet weight for framed pictures and box lids. Place the silk face down on the ironing board, cover with interfacing (adhesive side down) and press, following the manufacturer's instructions.

Making a Cushion Cover

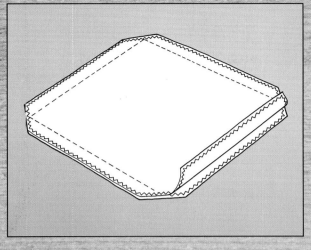

1 *Make a cushion cover from two pieces of fabric. Cut out the front and back pieces the same size, about 1.5cm (½in) larger all round than the finished size of the covers. Machine stitch the pieces together 1.5cm (½in) from the raw edge, leaving an opening along one side. Trim the corners to reduce bulk.*

2 *Turn the cover to the right side. Carefully poke out the corners with a knitting needle so they are square and press the cover. Insert the cushion pad and slipstitch the opening closed. You can use a different backing fabric from the painted silk front, but make sure that the two fabrics are the same weight.*

Hand Hemming

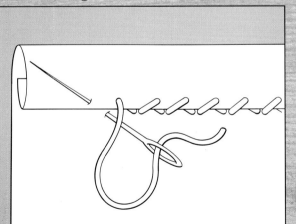

Fold over the fabric to make a narrow double hem and pin or tack in place. Using matching thread and a sewing needle, secure the thread inside the fold of the hem with a few tiny stitches. Take small slanting stitches through both the fabric and the hem fold in one movement. Pick up one or two fabric threads with each stitch and space the stitches evenly.

Buttonhole Stitch

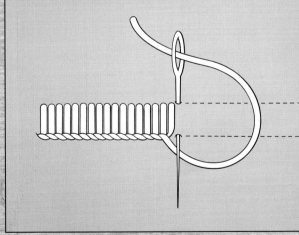

Buttonhole stitch is a looped stitch which can be used on fabric or worked over strands of threads to form a bar. Use buttonhole stitch to make the cufflinks on pages 48-49. Work buttonhole stitch from left to right, pulling the needle through so the point emerges over the top of the working thread. Work the stitches close together to completely cover the fabric.

Simply Scarves

Step out in style with a hand-painted silk scarf, just perfect for any occasion. The selection of scarves here have been carefully designed to cover the range of different silk painting techniques – so this is the place to start practising. Go for a dramatic look with a geometric scarf, or add a feminine touch with a pretty pansy scarf.

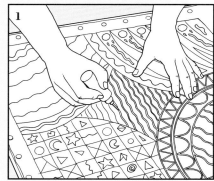

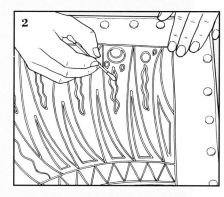

1 *All three designs are drawn freehand and then outlined directly on to the fabric. Use the close-up photographs as a guide and work freehand. Following the Silk Painting technique on page 14-15, pin the silk to the frame and draw the design with gold outliner, working from the centre outwards to avoid smudging. You may like to sign your name in outliner at the edge of the design. Allow the outliner to dry thoroughly before proceeding to the next step.*

▶ *These ethnic style scarves will add a magical touch to almost any outfit. The abstract designs are quick and easy to paint, and the rich gold colours add to the exclusive look.*

2 *Colour in the design using one colour of paint, again working from the centre outwards. Allow this colour to dry, then fill in the remaining colours one by one, allowing each colour to dry before proceeding to the next. For the scarf with the wide border, colour the border area with dark brown paint using the foam brush. Fix the paints following step 6 on page 14, or according to the manufacturer's instructions, then turn a narrow hem round each scarf and secure with a matching sewing thread, using the Hand Hemming technique on page 21.*

You Will Need:
Outliner bottle with fine nib
Large silk painting frame
3-point silk pins
Paintbrushes or cotton buds
Matching sewing thread

SCARF WITH CORNER PATTERNS:
1m (39in) square white 8
Habotai silk
Gold outliner
Silk paints in lemon yellow,
medium yellow, reddish orange,
light vermilion, russet brown,
dark brown, ochre, maytime
green, Parisian blue

SCARF WITH PATTERNED STRIPES:
75cm (30in) square white 8
Habotai silk
Gold outliner
Silk paints in lemon yellow,
russet brown, dark brown, ochre,
ultramarine blue, violet, black

SCARF WITH WIDE BORDER:
80cm (32in) square white 8
Habotai silk
Copper outliner
Silk paints in medium yellow,
vermilion red, russet brown, dark
brown, ochre, maytime green,
violet, black
25mm (1in) foam brush

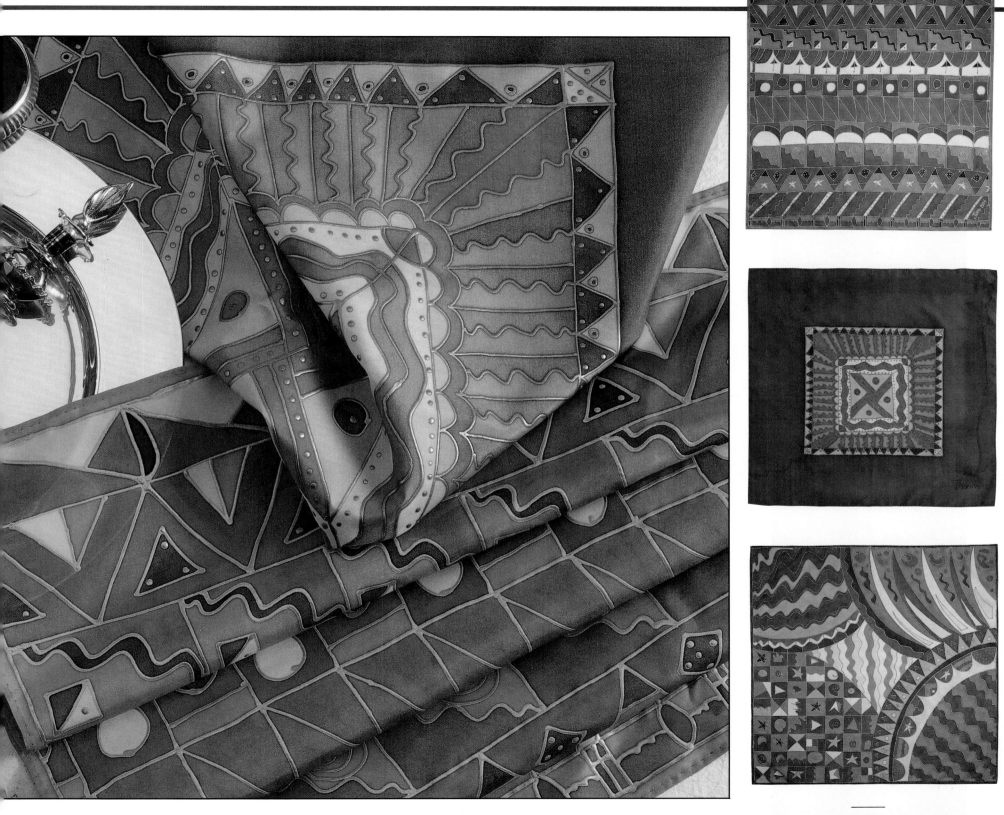

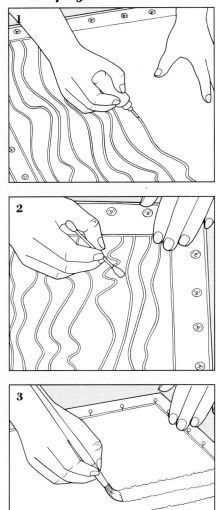

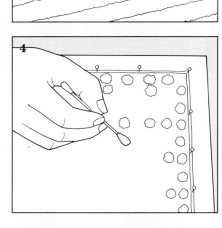

1 *For the wavy striped scarf, pin the fabric to the frame with 3-point silk pins. Following the Silk Painting technique on page 14-15 draw a line of clear outliner right round the scarf about 2.5cm (1in) from the raw edge to form the border strip. Outline wavy freehand stripes across the width of the scarf, making sure that the stripes join the border outline. Leave to dry.*

2 *Paint the design. Use one colour of paint and work from left to right across the frame. Allow this colour to dry, then fill in the remaining colours one by one, finishing with the border and allowing each colour to dry before proceeding to the next. Fix the paints following step 6 on page 14, or according to the manufacturer's instructions, then turn a narrow hem round the scarf and secure using the Hand Hemming technique on page 21.*

3 *Prepare the remaining two scarves by immersing them in salt solution following the technique given on page 16, and leave to dry. For the scarf with straight stripes, pin to the frame with map tacks inserted through the hem. Paint horizontal stripes across the scarf with the paintbrush. Paint all the yellow stripes first, then fill in the spaces between these stripes using the other colours. Fix the paint, then wash the scarf in cold water to remove the salt.*

4 *For the spotted scarf, pin to the frame using map tacks inserted through the hem. Dot random spots of lemon yellow, medium yellow and violet across the scarf using cotton buds, leaving plenty of space between the spots for the paint to spread. While the paint is still wet, dot pale blue and then ultramarine spots at the centre of each lemon spot. Finally, dot pale blue spots round the edge of the scarf. Fix the paint, then wash the scarf in cold water to remove salt.*

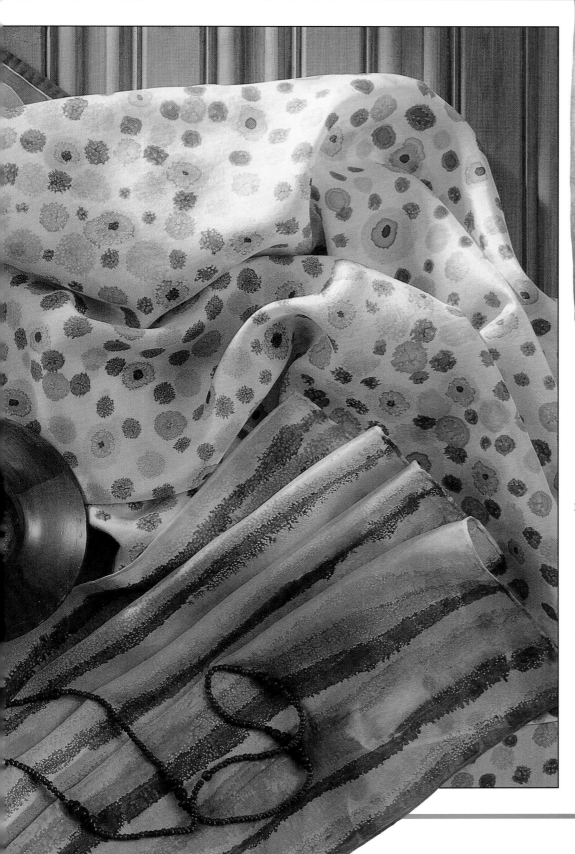

You Will Need:
Large silk painting frame
3-point silk pins or map tacks

SCARF WITH WAVY STRIPES:
50cm (20in) x 122cm (48in)
white 8 Habotai silk
Clear outliner
Outline bottle with fine nib
Silk paints in pale blue, yellow
green, medium yellow, lemon
yellow, reddish orange, pistachio
green, violet
Paintbrushes or cotton buds
Matching sewing thread

SCARF WITH STRAIGHT STRIPES:
55cm (22in) square white 5
Habotai silk scarf
Salt solution
Silk paints in lemon yellow,
reddish orange, pale blue, violet
Large paintbrush

SCARF WITH SPOTS:
90cm (36in) square white 8
Habotai silk scarf
Salt solution
Silk paints in lemon yellow,
medium yellow, pale blue,
ultramarine blue, violet
Cotton buds

▲ *Create a softer look by using
salt treated fabric for silk
painting. Here, delicately
spreading striped and spotted
patterns are quick and easy to
create on ready-made scarves.*

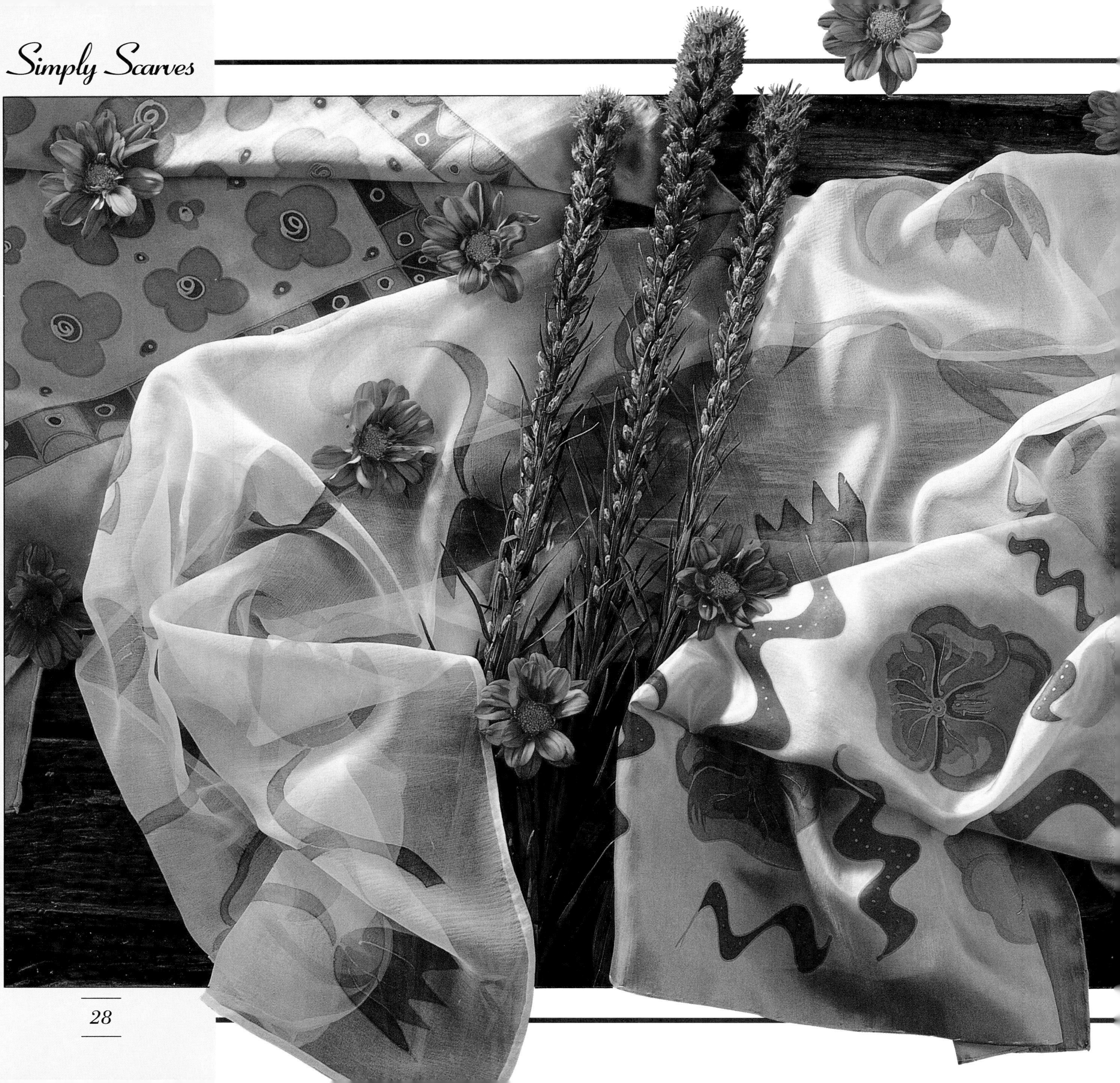

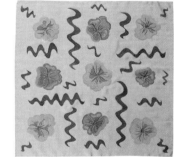

▲ *Heavier fabrics are perfect for making into everyday scarves, and can then be used throughout the year.*

You Will Need:
Outliner bottle with a fine nib
Large silk painting frame
Paintbrushes or cotton buds
Fade-away embroidery marker

SCARF WITH BORDER:
55cm (22in) square lavender
8 Habotai silk scarf
Pink, clear and gold outliner
Silk paints in yellow, maytime green, pale pink, lavender, raspberry, violet
Map tacks

SCARF WITH PANSIES:
55cm (22in) square pale pink
8 Habotai silk scarf
Purple and clear outliner
Silk paints in lemon yellow, mandarin yellow, orange, rose pink, reddish violet, violet, purple
Map tacks

SCARF WITH TULIPS:
43cm (17in) x 122cm (48in) white silk chiffon
Clear outliner
Silk paints in yellow, rose pink, olive green
3-point silk pins
Matching sewing thread

◀ *Single tulip motifs scattered over a filmy white chiffon scarf make a delicate summer wrap - ideal for a special occasion.*

1 *All three designs can be drawn freehand on the fabric with an embroidery marker, or you may prefer to trace off the template for the tulip design given on page 102, and transfer it to the silk following the technique on page 20. Pin the lavender scarf to the frame with map tacks inserted through the hem. Following the Silk Painting technique on page 14-15, outline the border round the scarf using pink outliner. Allow to dry, then draw flower shapes and small circles with clear outliner scattering them across the centre of the scarf. Allow to dry, draw a gold spiral flower centre, and place a gold dot in each circle.*

2 *Using the close-up photograph as a guide, colour in the border pattern, flowers and circles using a paintbrush or cotton buds. Use one colour at a time and work from the centre outwards. Allow each colour to dry before painting the next. Fix the paint.*

3 *For the pansy design, pin the pink scarf to the frame using map pins. Using clear outliner, draw nine evenly spaced pansy flowers across the scarf, then draw scroll shapes in between. The close-up photograph will help with positioning. Allow to dry, then draw spiral flower centres and radiating lines using purple outliner at the centre of each pansy. Also, add a line of purple dots along each scroll shape and allow to dry. Colour in the motifs and fix the paint.*

4 *To make the tulip scarf, pin the fabric to the frame using 3-point silk pins and draw randomly spaced tulip motifs across the fabric using clear outliner. Allow to dry, then colour in the tulip motifs and fix the paints. Finally, turn a narrow hem round the edge and secure with hand hemming following the technique given on page 21, and using a matching sewing thread.*

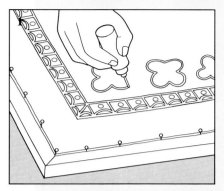

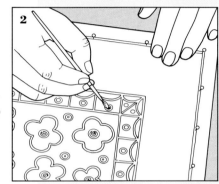

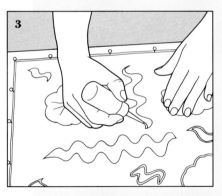

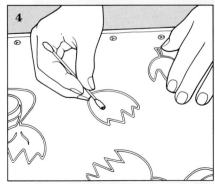

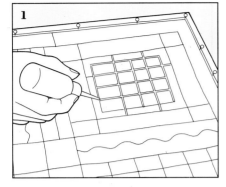

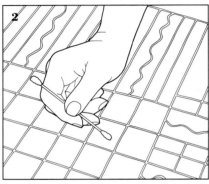

1 *The outlined designs are drawn freehand on to the fabric with an embroidery marker. Pin the large scarf to the frame with map tacks inserted through the hem. Following the Silk Painting technique on page 14-15, outline the border pattern and corner motifs round the edge of the scarf using clear outliner. Work from left to right round the edge of the scarf. Allow to dry, then outline a chequerboard pattern to fill the central portion of the scarf, making each check about 3cm (1¹/₄in) square. Allow to dry.*

2 *Using the close-up photograph as a colour guide, colour in the design. Use one colour of paint at a time and work from the centre outwards, to avoid smudging. Allow each colour to dry before proceeding to the next. Fix the paints.*

You Will Need:
Large
silk painting frame
Map tacks
Paintbrushes
or cotton buds
Fade-away
embroidery marker

CHECKED SCARF WITH BORDER:
90cm (36in) square white 8
Habotai silk scarf
Clear outliner
Outliner bottle with fine nib
Silk paints in lemon yellow,
reddish orange, light vermilion
red, mid green, pine green, violet,
dark ultramarine blue

TARTAN SCARF:
55cm (22in) square white 5
Habotai silk scarf
Gold outliner
Outliner bottle with fine nib
Silk paints in lemon yellow,
reddish orange, light vermilion
red, mid green, pine green, violet,
dark ultramarine blue.

TARTAN SCARF WITH IRREGULAR
PATTERN:
55cm (22in) square white 8
Habotai silk scarf
Salt solution
Silk paints in lemon yellow, light
vermilion red, dark ultramarine
blue

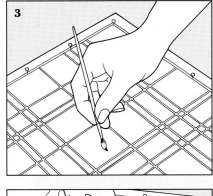

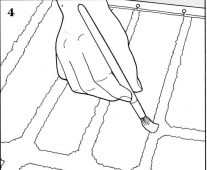

3 *For the tartan design, pin the scarf to the frame using map tacks. Outline the repeating tartan pattern across the scarf with gold outliner using the close-up photograph to help you space the gold lines and working from the centre of the scarf outwards to avoid smudging. Allow to dry, then colour in the tartan pattern and fix the paints.*

4 *For the scarf with the irregular tartan pattern, prepare the scarf by immersing in salt solution following the technique given on page 16, and allow to dry. Pin to the frame using map tacks. Paint horizontal and vertical stripes of lemon yellow across the scarf using a large paintbrush. Then repeat with blue and red stripes. Fix the paints, then wash the scarf in cold water to remove the salt.*

◄ *Bold check and tartan patterns look stunning worked across large areas. Choose bright paints to add a dash of colour to any outfit.*

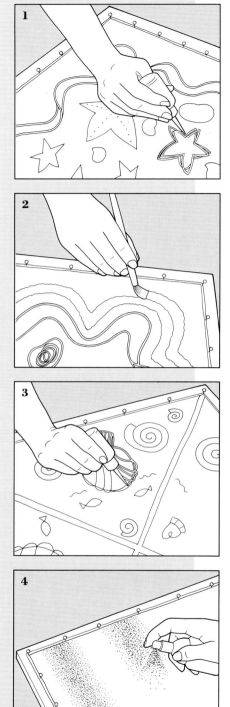

1 *All three designs are drawn freehand directly on the fabric with an embroidery marker before outlining, or you may prefer to trace off the shell templates given on page 102, and transfer these to the silk following the technique on page 20. To make the starfish scarf, pin the scarf to the frame with map tacks. Following the Silk Painting technique on page 14-15, outline the wavy border round the scarf using clear outliner. Allow to dry, then draw starfish and shell shapes with clear outliner, scattering them across the central area of the scarf. Allow to dry, then draw gold and copper lines round each starfish close to but not covering the existing outlines. Add copper dots along the arms of each starfish. Finally, add gold spirals to decorate each shell. Allow to dry completely.*

2 *Using the close-up photograph as a colour guide, colour in the ochre border using a wide brush and allowing each stripe of paint to dry before applying the next. Colour in the remaining border stripe and the starfish and shells. Use one colour of paint at a time and work from the centre of the scarf outwards, to avoid smudging. Allow each colour to dry before proceeding to the next. Finally, colour in the background with dark blue paint, applying it with a large brush and leaving some areas white. Allow to dry, then fill in the white areas with dark green. Fix the paints following step 6, on page 14, or according to the manufacturer's instructions.*

3 *For the shell design, pin the peach scarf to the frame. Using copper outliner, draw double diagonal lines across the scarf to divide it into four triangles. Add scallop shells and spiral shells and tiny fish, all drawn in copper outliner. Allow to dry, colour in the motifs, then fix the paints.*

You Will Need:
Outliner bottle with fine nib
Large silk painting frame
Map tacks
Paintbrushes or cotton buds
Fade-away embroidery marker

SCARF WITH STARFISH DESIGN:
90cm (36in) square white
8 Habotai silk scarf
Clear, gold and copper outliner
Silk paints in peach, salmon pink, Parisian blue, deep green, azure blue, turquoise, ochre

SCARF WITH SHELL DESIGN:
55cm (22in) square peach
8 Habotai silk scarf
Copper outliner
Silk paints in salmon pink, orchid pink, old gold, ochre, oriental green, turquoise

SCARF WITH FISH DESIGN:
40cm (16in) x 150cm (59in)
white 5 Habotai silk scarf
Clear, green and blue outliner
Silk paints in primary yellow, old gold, oriental green, turquoise, bright blue
Paint diffuser or atomiser bottle

4 *To make the fish scarf, pin the scarf to the frame with map tacks and spray graduating strips of oriental green, bright blue and turquoise across the width of scarf using a paint diffuser or atomiser bottle. Spray the colour very lightly and don't worry if the paint spatters as this adds to the undersea effect. Allow to dry, then outline randomly spaced fish motifs across the fabric using clear outliner. Add wavy lines and dots to represent eyes using blue and green outliner. Colour in the fish motifs and fix the paints.*

▲ Fish, shells and starfish
give a seaside theme to a pair of
silk scarves. Contrasting colours of
metallic outliner and a delicate
sprayed background add to the
charm of the simple fish-shapes
used on the longer scarf.

Simply Scarves

You Will Need:

WAX CRACKLE SCARF:
55cm (22in) square yellow 8
Habotai silk scarf
Dark grey silk paint
Silk painting frame
Map tacks
Cotton wool
Clothes peg
Batik wax
Small heatproof bowl
Old saucepan
Old paintbrush
Scrap paper or newspaper

SCRUNCH PAINTED SCARF:
61cm (24in) x 150cm (59in)
white 8 Habotai silk
Silk paints in ochre, dark ochre,
reddish orange, sand, pastel
yellow, smoky blue
Eye droppers
Polythene sheet
Matching sewing thread

▶ *Three different techniques —
wax crackle, scrunch painting
and spraying create soft, subtle
patterns on a trio of silk scarves.*

SCARF WITH SPRAYED PATTERNS:
90cm (36in) square white 8
Habotai silk scarf
Silk paints in russet brown,
lemon yellow, mandarin yellow,
maytime green, orange
Scraps of thin card
Paint diffuser or atomiser bottle
Newspaper

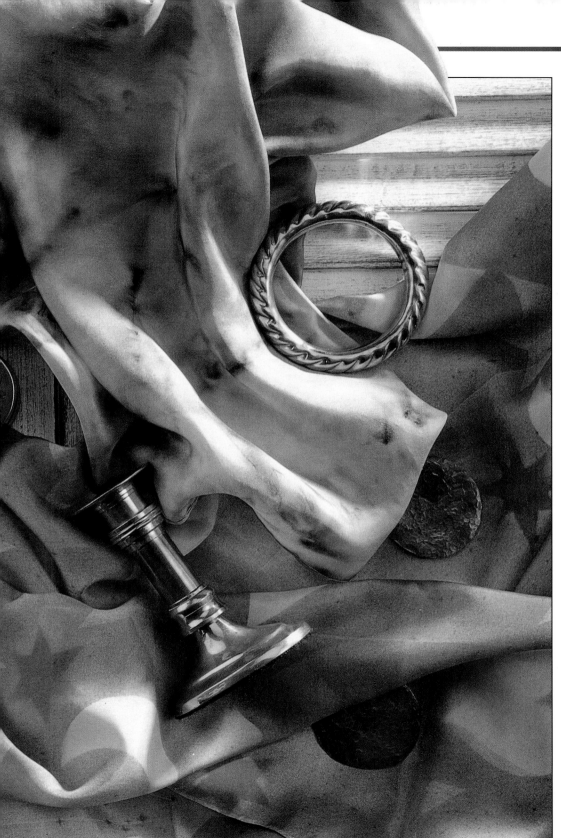

1 *To make the wax crackle scarf, pin the yellow scarf to the frame with map tacks and follow the Wax Crackle technique given on page 19, rubbing dark grey paint into the cracked wax. Remove the wax, following step 4 on page 19, wash the scarf in warm water and detergent to remove any last traces of wax.*

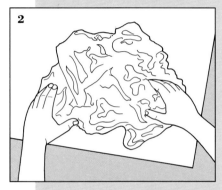

2 *To make the scrunch painted scarf, wash the fabric to remove any dressing and wring out gently to remove surplus water. Spread a large polythene sheet on a flat surface and place the wet silk on the sheet, scrunching it with your hands. Mop up any pools of water from the polythene.*

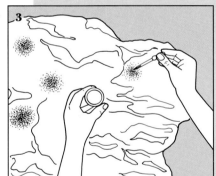

3 *Working colour by colour, apply splodges of paint randomly across the scrunched fabric using a separate eye dropper for each colour. Allow the colours to blend and mingle, and make sure that there are no areas of white fabric left uncoloured. Allow the fabric to dry before lifting off the polythene. Fix the paint according to the manufacturer's instructions. Turn a narrow hem and secure with hand hemming.*

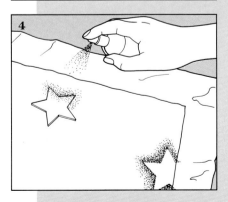

4 *For the scarf with sprayed decoration, lay the pressed scarf on a flat surface covered with newspaper and spray very lightly across the scarf with russet brown in a diffuser or atomiser bottle. Cut star, circle, heart, triangle and half-moon shapes out of card. Cut a smaller star shape out of the centre of a square of card. Templates for all these shapes are given on page 102. Lay the cut-out shapes at random on the fabric and spray with russet brown to make shaped outlines. Allow to dry, rearrange the shapes on the scarf and spray again with lemon yellow and yellow. Repeat with maytime green and allow to dry. Finally, place the stencils on the fabric and spray with orange to make solid star shapes, moving the stencils across the fabric.*

Finishing Touches

Add a dash of elegance to any outfit with superb silk painted accessories. Make stylish jewellery from cleverly wrapped bangles to classic brooches. Jazz up a favourite shirt with stunning buttons and cuff links, or simply add a hand-painted tie to give an instant designer look. There's even a 'raining cats and dogs' brolly for those wet weather days.

Finishing Touches

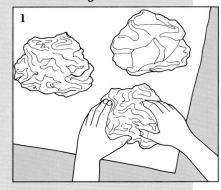

1 *To make the scrunch painted handkerchiefs. Wash the handkerchiefs to remove any dressing and wring out gently to remove surplus water. Spread a large polythene sheet on a flat surface and place one wet handkerchief on the sheet scrunching it evenly with your hands. Repeat with the remaining handkerchiefs. Mop up any pools of water from the polythene.*

You Will Need:
SCRUNCH PAINTED HANDKERCHIEFS:
Cream, yellow, white and pale blue spun silk handkerchiefs
Silk paints in lemon yellow, mid yellow, mandarin orange, deep orange, vermilion red, carmine red
Eye droppers
Polythene sheet

▶ *Quick to make these wax crackle handkerchiefs have a very delicate feathery look.*

▼ *The scrunch painted handkerchiefs have been decorated in a rainbow of colours.*

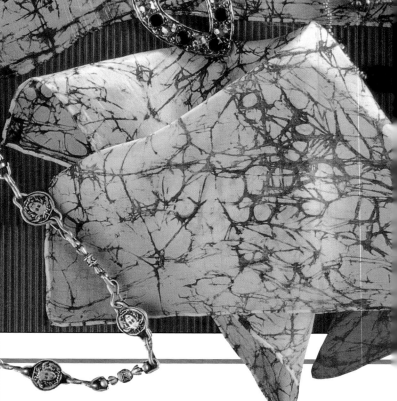

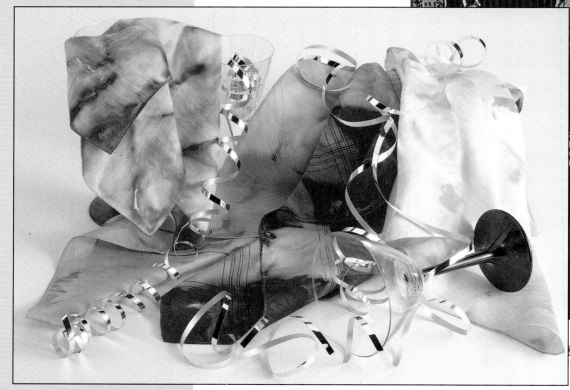

You Will Need:

WAX CRACKLE
HANDKERCHIEFS:
Cream, White and
orange Habotai
or spun silk
handkerchiefs
Small silk
painting frame
Silk paints in
khaki, dark grey,
red
Map tacks
Batik wax
Small heatproof bowl
Old saucepan
Old paintbrush
Cotton wool
Clothes peg
Scrap paper or
newspaper

1 *The wax crackle handkerchiefs are decorated individually, while several scrunch painted handkerchiefs can be decorated at the same time. For the wax crackle decoration, pin a handkerchief to a small frame using map tacks inserted through the hem. Follow the Wax Crackle technique given on page 19, apply melted wax to the fabric and allow to set. Remove from the frame and crumple the handkerchief in your hands.*

2 *Pin the handkerchief back in the frame and rub paint into the surface with a ball of cotton wool held in a clothes peg. Use khaki or dark grey for the white and cream handkerchiefs and red for the orange one. Remove the wax following step 4 on page 19, and wash in warm water and detergent to remove any remaining traces of wax.*

2 *Working colour by colour, apply splodges of paint randomly on the scrunched handkerchiefs, using a separate eye dropper for each colour. Allow the colours to blend and leave some areas of fabric uncoloured. Use lemon yellow and mandarin orange on the blue and white handkerchiefs; mid yellow, deep orange, vermilion red and carmine red on the yellow and white handkerchiefs. Allow the paint to dry before removing from the polythene, then fix the paint.*

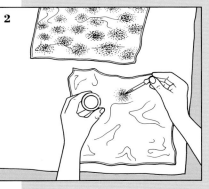

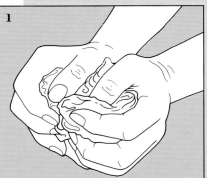

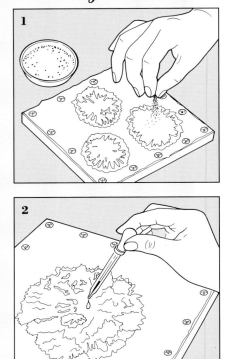

1 For the blue and turquoise pendants, pin a piece of white silk on the frame with 3-point silk pins. Working individually for each item quickly paint a circle of colour on the silk, and before the paint dries, sprinkle with salt. Allow to dry, brush off the salt and fix the colour following step 6 on page 14. Wash to remove the salt. When dry back with interfacing following the technique on page 20, and mount in the silver frames following the manufacturer's instructions. Repeat with pink Habotai to make the pink bow brooch.

2 For the round and oval brooches with purple and yellow patterns, pin a piece of silk in the frame with 3-point silk pins. Quickly drop spots of yellow, violet, turquoise green, turquoise and salmon pink on the silk using a separate eye dropper for each colour. Place the spots close together so the colours blend and, while the paint is still wet,

sprinkle the whole area with sea salt. Fix, wash and apply interfacing following the technique on page 20. Place the silver mounts on the patterned silk and move around to help you select the most pleasing areas of pattern. Mount the silk in the frame following the manufacturer's instructions.

▲ Small pieces of silk painted fabric makes wonderful items of jewellery. Here, the fabric has been prepared using the dry salt technique.

You Will Need:
Scraps of white and fuchsia pink 8 Habotai silk
Salt solution and dry salt
Silk paints in turquoise green, turquoise, bright blue, violet, purple, salmon pink, raspberry, yellow, black
Silk painting frame
3-point silk pins
Paintbrushes
Silver-plated jewellery mounts from Framecraft
(Details on page 108.)
Iron-on pelmet interfacing

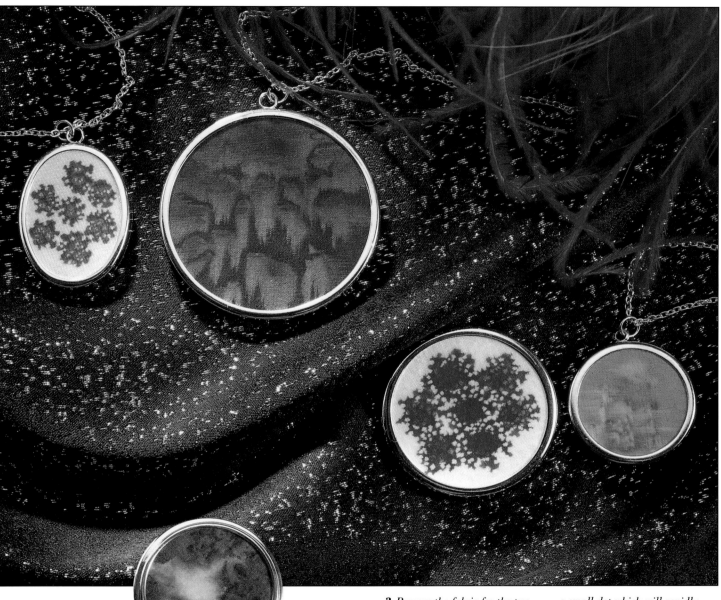

▲ *Mount the finished pieces in silver-plated brooch and pendant mounts, available from specialist stores. The items here have been painted after the fabric has been treated by being immersed in salt.*

3 *Prepare the fabric for the two remaining groups of jewellery by immersing two small pieces of white Habotai silk in the salt solution following the technique given on page 16. Leave to dry. Pin one piece to the frame with 3-point silk pins. To make the small blue pendant and pink brooch with snowflake patterns load a small paintbrush with paint and lightly dab the brush point on the treated fabric to make*

a small dot which will rapidly spread to make a snowflake shape. Add six more dots round the first to make a circular pattern. Fix the paint, then mount the jewellery following the manufacturer's instructions.

4 *Pin the second piece of silk to the frame with 3-point silk pins. To make the striped pendant and brooch, load a small paintbrush with paint and lightly draw across the fabric to make straight or curved stripes. Make further stripes close to the first. For the remaining bow brooch, make three dots close to each other, then press the loaded brush flat on the silk and repeat to make a radiating pattern. Fix the paint.*

Finishing Touches

You Will Need:
Large piece of white 8
Habotai silk, about 90cm (36in)
square
Large silk painting frame
Clear and copper outliner
Outliner bottle with fine nib
Silk paints in yellow, scarlet,
grass green, blue green, bright
blue
Paintbrushes or cotton buds
Rotary cutter or sharp scissors
PVA craft medium
Polythene sheet
Old paintbrush
Saucer or flat dish

BANGLES:
Plastic bangles in varying widths

NECKLACES:
Knitting needles
Petroleum jelly
Wood, glass and metal beads
Narrow leather thongs

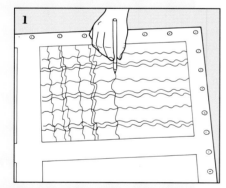

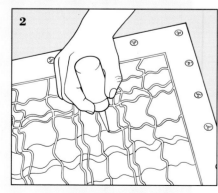

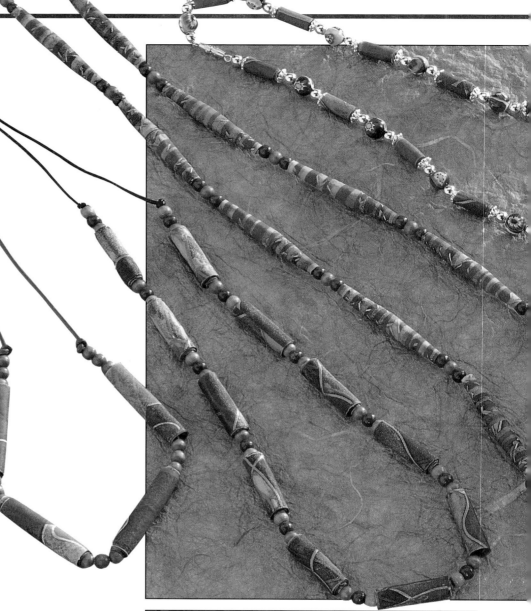

1 *To decorate the fabric, pin the silk to the frame with 3-point silk pins. Using the embroidery marker, divide the silk into four areas, allowing about 2.5cm (1in) between each one. Mark out a different geometric pattern in each area. You can use the close-up photographs as a guide or you may decide to design your own pattern.*

2 *Following the Silk Painting technique on page 14-15, outline each area using either clear or copper outliner. Allow to dry, then outline the pattern marked in each area using either clear or copper outliner or a combination of the two. Allow to dry thoroughly.*

▶ *Use the patterns shown in the close-up photographs to paint the fabric or design your own patterns for the wrapped beads.*

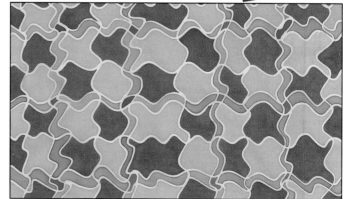

3 *Colour in the outlined patterns using a paintbrush or cotton buds, and allow each colour to dry before proceeding to the next. Fix the paints following step 6 on page 14, or according to the manufacturer's instructions. Use a rotary cutter or sharp scissors to cut the fabric into strips. Cut the strips between 1.5cm (¹/₂in) and 5cm (2in) wide, tapering some of the strips at one end. Make the strips about 30cm (12in) long. Vary the effect by cutting some strips on the straight grain and others on the cross.*

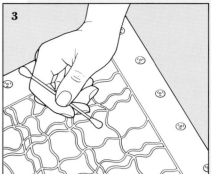

4 *Place the polythene sheet on a flat surface. Pour some PVA craft medium into a saucer and dilute it with water until the consistency is like thin cream. Lay several cut strips on the polythene and brush the diluted PVA along them with an old paintbrush, working from end to end until the painted fabric is completely saturated.*

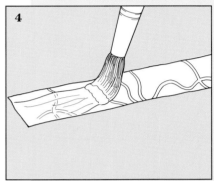

5 *To wrap the bangles take a strip of PVA saturated fabric and wrap it round the bangle, overlapping the layers by about 1.5cm (¹/₂in). When the first strip is used up, add another and repeat until the bangle is covered with fabric. Give the wrapped bangle a coat of diluted PVA and leave on the polythene until completely dry.*

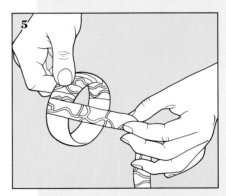

6 *To make beads, coat a knitting needle with petroleum jelly. Wrap a PVA saturated strip of fabric tightly and evenly round the knitting needle. Remove the bead from the needle and leave on the polythene to dry. Repeat to make several beads from each piece of patterned silk. For the tapered strips begin wrapping at the blunt end and finish with the pointed end. Thread the finished beads on to narrow leather thonging, separating the silk beads with wood, glass or metal beads to vary the effect. Tie the thong ends in a knot. Alternatively, thread on to a special bead thread and add a jewellery fastening to the ends.*

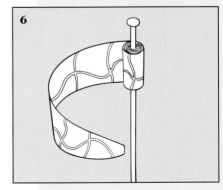

▲ *Using the techniques borrowed from papercrafts, boldly patterned silk is used to make items of fun jewellery. Wooden, metal and glass beads complement the painted silk.*

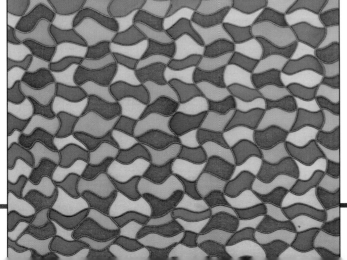

Finishing Touches

You Will Need:
Polythene sheet and Eye droppers

BLUE AND YELLOW TIE:
Ready-made white silk jacquard tie
Silk paints in mandarin yellow, bright blue, silver grey

YELLOW AND GREY TIE:
Ready-made white silk twill tie
Gold outliner
Outliner bottle with fine nib
Silk paints in yellow, silver grey
Silver opaque fabric paint

TIE WITH SILVER SPIRALS:
Ready-made white Habotai silk tie
Silver outliner
Outliner bottle with fine nib
Silk paints in mandarin yellow, orange, blue grey

BOW TIES:
Ready-made twill Habotai silk bow ties
Silk paints in bright blue, deep turquoise

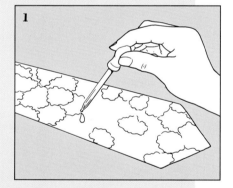

1 *To make the blue and yellow tie, lay the polythene sheet on a flat surface and place the tie on the sheet, right side up. Using separate eye droppers for each colour, drop spots of mandarin yellow, bright blue and silver grey on to the tie. Allow the colours to blend into each other so there are no white areas showing. Allow to dry, then fix the colours following step 6 on page 14, or according to the manufacturer's instructions.*

▶ *Ready-made ties and bow-ties are available in a wide range of silk fabric, including twill and fancy weaves such as jacquard. Here, the ties have been quickly decorated with bold splashes of paint.*

2 *For the yellow and grey design, work in the same way as step 1, but drop spots of yellow at random on the tie and allow to dry for about 5 minutes. Then drop spots of silver grey between the yellow until the white background is covered. Paint spots of silver paint at the centre of the yellow areas and allow to dry. Using gold outliner, squiggle lines of gold across the tie and add a dot of gold to the silver spots. Allow to dry, then fix the paints.*

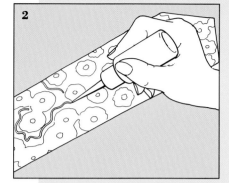

3 *To make the tie with silver spirals, drop spots of yellow and orange over the tie. Allow to dry, then drop spots of blue grey to cover the remaining areas of background fabric. Allow to dry, then make a small spiral at the centre of each orange spot using silver outliner. Allow to dry, then fix the paint.*

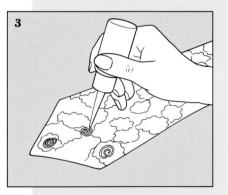

4 *To decorate the bow ties, place them on a polythene sheet. Drop spots of bright blue and deep turquoise on to the ties and allow the colours to run into each other until the background is covered. Allow to dry and fix the paints.*

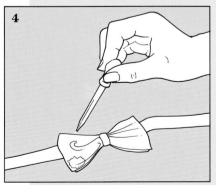

45

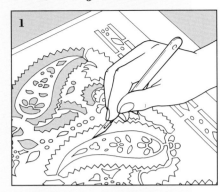

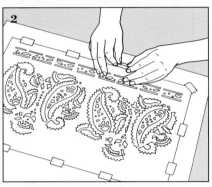

▶ *This luxurious evening wrap and matching drawstring bag are the perfect accessories for a night on the town. To make your evening wrap exclusive use a different stencil or another colour combination.*

1 *Trace off the paisley template given on page 102, enlarging it to the correct size and transfer the design onto the stencil card. Place the card on the cutting mat and carefully cut along the template lines with a craft knife.*

2 *Place the polythene sheet on a flat surface. Position one end of the wrap fabric on the polythene and secure with masking tape. Place the stencil over the fabric so the base of the design is about 8cm (3in) from the raw edge along the short end. Secure the stencil on the silk with masking tape.*

You Will Need:
55cm x 2m (22 x 80in)
terracotta washed silk to make
the wrap
Two pieces 22 x 30cm
(8 $\frac{1}{2}$ x 12in) of the same fabric to
make the bag
Gold opaque fabric paint
Small piece of natural sponge
Saucer or flat dish
38 x 51cm (15 x 20in) piece of
oiled stencil card
Craft knife and cutting mat
Polythene sheet
Masking tape
120cm (48in) narrow gold cord
Four ready-made gold tassels
8cm (3in) long
Matching sewing thread

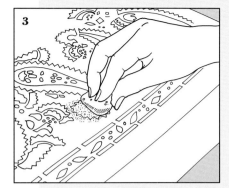

3 *Transfer a small amount of fabric paint into the saucer. Dip the sponge into the paint and apply to the stencil with a dabbing movement. Repeat across the stencil, taking care not to overload the sponge with paint. Carefully remove the stencil and allow the paint to dry. Repeat the design at the opposite end of the fabric. Allow to dry, then fix the paint according to the manufacturer's instructions.*

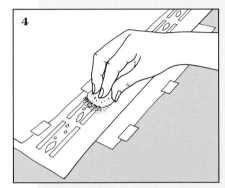

4 *Repeat the stencilling process on the two bag pieces, but this time mask off the stencil by sticking a piece of paper across the paisley design with masking tape so that just the narrow border can be seen. Stencil the border across the width of the bag, about 4cm (1¹/₂in) from the raw edge. Allow to dry, then fix the paint.*

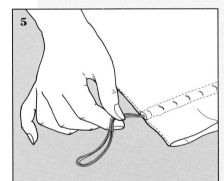

5 *Turn a narrow hem round the wrap and machine stitch with matching thread. Place the two bag pieces together with right sides facing and machine round three sides, leaving a small gap in the stitching about 11cm (4¹/₂in) from the top edge of the bag. Turn to the right side, fold over about 6.5cm (2¹/₂in) along the top edge and work two rows of machine stitching round the bag about 4cm (1¹/₂in) and 5cm (2in) away from the fold to make a casing corresponding with the gap left in the stitching. Cut the cord into two lengths and thread through the casing. Knot the ends together and pull the loops through the casing, so that one loop protrudes at either side of the bag.*

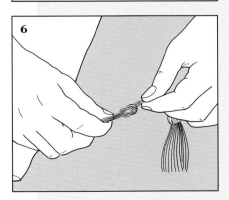

6 *Trim the loops on two of the tassels down to about 1cm (¹/₂in) and stitch a tassel securely to each of the lower corners of the bag using matching thread. To finish off the cords, knot the long loops of the remaining tassels on to the two cord loops protruding from the bag. Pull the loops to close the bag.*

Finishing Touches

1 With all these designs, paint several at the same time on one piece of fabric, leaving about 2.5cm (1in) between each one. · Remove the piece of backing card from one of the button moulds, place it on the silk and draw round it with a soft pencil. Repeat several times until you have the correct size of circle for each button and cufflink you wish to make. Remember that you will need four circles of silk for every pair of cufflinks you make.

2 Pin the silk to the frame with 3-point silk pins. Using the colour photographs as a guide and following the Silk Painting technique on page 14-15, draw the designs freehand on the silk with the correct colour of outliner. Remember to outline round the circle about 1cm (¹/₂in) outside the pencil line to prevent the colours from spreading too far. Allow the outliner to dry completely.

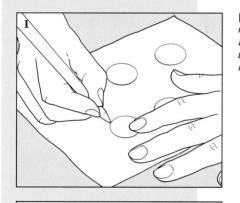

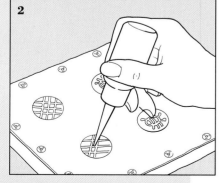

▶ Use up small scraps of silk to make these buttons and cuff links. Button moulds can be bought in the haberdashery departments of most large stores.

You Will Need:
White 8 Habotai silk
Small silk painting frame
Outliner bottle with fine nib
Small paintbrush
Lightweight iron-on interfacing

BEETLE BUTTONS:
Six 29mm (1¼in) button moulds
with brass rims
Clear outliner
Silk paints in oriental green,
turquoise, purple

BUTTERFLY CUFF LINKS:
Four 19mm (⅞in) button moulds
with brass rims for each set
Pink outliner
Silk paints in black, turquoise
Black and pink stranded
embroidery thread
Tapestry needle

CHECKED BUTTONS:
Six 29mm (1¼in) button moulds
with brass rims
Clear outliner
Silk paints in yellow, oriental
green, turquoise, raspberry pink,
purple

STRIPED CUFF LINKS:
Four 22mm (⅞in) button moulds
with brass rims
Clear outliner
Silk paints in yellow, oriental
green, turquoise, raspberry pink,
purple
Purple stranded embroidery
thread
Tapestry needle

GEOMETRIC BUTTONS:
Six 29mm (1¼in) button moulds
with brass rims
Clear outliner
Silk paints in oriental green,
turquoise, raspberry pink, purple

GEOMETRIC CUFF LINKS:
Four 22mm (⅞in) button moulds
with brass rims
Clear outliner
Silk paints in yellow, oriental
green, raspberry pink, purple
Purple stranded embroidery
thread
Tapestry needle

3 *Using the photographs as a colour guide, colour in the designs with a small paintbrush. Use one colour of paint at a time and work from the centre of the silk outwards, to avoid smudging. Allow each colour to dry, before proceeding to the next. Fix the paints following step 6 on page 14, or according to the manufacturer's instructions.*

4 *Back each piece of painted silk with interfacing before cutting out the circles along the pencil outlines. Assemble the layers of the mould on a flat surface – holder, brass rim, fabric (right side downwards), metal centre, back and finally the pusher. Push firmly downwards to secure the layers.*

5 *To make the cufflink, use six strands of embroidery thread to make the embroidered link joining the two buttons together. To begin, thread the needle with a 45cm (18in) length of thread and knot the free end securely round the loop on the back of one button.*

6 *Strand the thread three or four times between the two buttons to make a firm foundation for the link. Embroider over the strands using the Buttonhole Stitch technique on page 21, working the stitches close together to completely cover the strands. Finish off the thread end securely.*

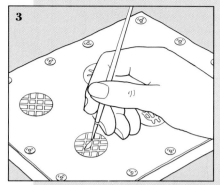

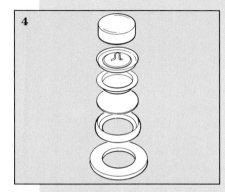

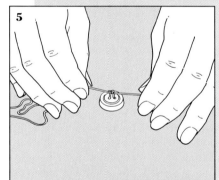

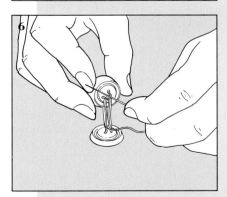

Finishing Touches

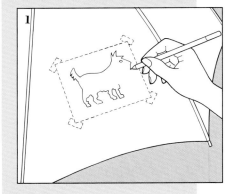

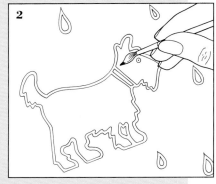

You Will Need:
Ready-made silk umbrella
Clear outliner
Outliner bottle with fine nib
Silk paints in blue grey, black,
carmine red, mandarin yellow,
bright blue, turquoise
Paintbrushes
Fade-away embroidery marker

1 Trace off the cat and dog templates given on page 102. You will need four tracings of each template. Cut round the tracings about 2.5cm (1in) from the edge of the designs. Tape the tracings to the wrong side of the umbrella, one tracing to each panel, making sure that the designs are used alternately. The base of each design should be about 10cm (4in) from the edge of the panel. Trace the designs on to the silk with the marker and dot raindrop shapes at random about the cats and dogs.

2 Outline the designs with clear outliner, working a panel at a time and letting one section dry before moving on to the next. Using the close-up photographs as a guide, colour in the designs using a paintbrush. Allow to dry, then place the umbrella on an ironing board and carefully press each panel from the wrong side to fix the paint.

▶ Cats and dogs look out from this charming umbrella patterned with raindrops. Spray the finished article with water repellent.

▲ *Cats and dogs are fairly easy motifs to draw freehand, but for added ease these motifs are given in the templates section on page 102.*

Stepping Out

From perfect party tops to sarongs for the beach, silk is the
most natural fabric for any occasion.
Add flair to a simple T shirt with a silk-painted motif,
or make a shirt from silk then paint it
with wacky stencilled stars.
You could even use the ideas here to design
your own special outfits
for daytime or evening wear.

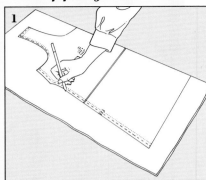

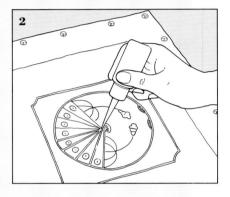

1 *Press the silk. Cut out the paper pattern pieces. Lay the front pattern piece on the silk and draw round the edge with the embroidery marker, turn the pattern over and continue drawing round the edge until you have the complete front shape marked out. Cut out a rectangle of silk containing the front outline plus a margin of about 5cm (2in) round the edge and pin to the frame with 3-point pins.*

2 *Trace off the fan template given on page 102 and transfer it to the front three times, using the photograph as a positioning guide. Following the Silk Painting steps on page 14-15, outline with silver outliner and colour in the fan motifs with a paintbrush. Allow to dry, then fix the paint following step 6 on page 14, or according to the manufacturer's instructions. Make up the garment using matching sewing thread.*

You Will Need:
Paper pattern for sleeveless blouse
Bright pink 8 Habotai silk
Silver outliner
Outliner bottle with fine nib
Large silk painting frame
Silk paints in old gold, carmine red, purple, pistachio green, bright blue
Paintbrush
Matching sewing thread
Fade-away embroidery marker

▶ *An Art Deco-inspired pattern of fans decorates a simple sleeveless evening top. Choose a pastel colour for the background fabric for a traditional effect, or use paler colours against a dark background.*

Stepping Out

▶ *A classically styled man's shirt
takes on a whole new look when
decorated with gold and silver
stencilled stars.*

56

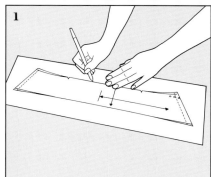

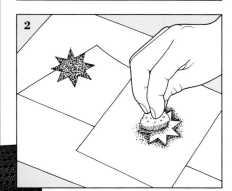

1 *Trace off the two star templates on page 102, transfer to the stencil card and cut out with the craft knife. Cut out the paper pattern pieces. Lay the collar, yoke, front band and cuff pieces on the fabric, leaving a gap of 10cm (4in) between each piece. Draw round each piece with the pencil, remembering to mark out the cuff piece twice. Cut out a rectangle of fabric containing each piece plus 5cm (2in) round the edge. Place the fabric on a flat surface covered with paper.*

2 *Transfer some silver paint into the saucer, and place the larger star stencil on the fabric. Dip the sponge into the paint and apply to the stencil with a dabbing movement. Remove the stencil, and leave to dry. Reposition the stencil and repeat across the fabric, leaving spaces for the smaller stars. Repeat the process with the gold paint, this time using the small star stencil. Allow the paint to dry, then fix the paint. Make up the garment.*

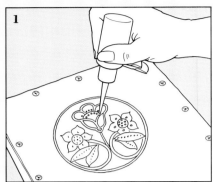

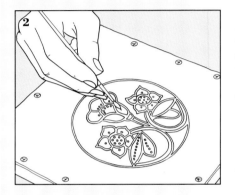

1 *Trace off the template for the T shirt motif on page 103, and transfer it, following the technique on page 20, to the white silk. Pin the silk to the frame with 3-point silk pins and following the Silk Painting technique on page 14-15, outline the design with copper outliner. Allow to dry.*

2 *Using the photograph as a colour guide, colour in the design with a paintbrush. Paint a narrow strip with deep turquoise just outside the outlined circle. Allow to dry, then fix the paint. Iron a piece of fusible bonding web on to the wrong side of the motif and cut out the motif close to the copper outline. Peel off the backing paper and position the motif on the right side of the T shirt. Press in position following the manufacturer's instructions.*

You Will Need:
Ready-made deep turquoise
green silk T shirt
Small square of white 8
Habotai silk
Copper outliner
Outliner bottle with fine nib
Small silk painting frame
3-point silk pins
Silk paints in emerald green,
bright blue, bronze, deep
turquoise
Paintbrush
Fusible bonding web

▶ *Here a painted silk medallion featuring a Art Nouveau floral design is applied to the front of a silk T shirt.*

Stepping Out

► A large hemmed rectangle of washed silk is scrunch painted. Here, bright summery shades of yellow, green and turquoise are used, but other colours would also work well.

You Will Need:
112 x 150cm (45 x 60in) white washed silk
Silk paints in mid yellow, oriental green and turquoise
Eye droppers
Large polythene sheet
Matching sewing thread

For a neat look it is best to tie the sarong using the knot you would use when tying a man's tie, except that you should pass the fabric over the top of the knot.

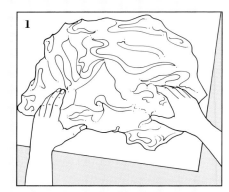

1 Wash the fabric to remove any dressing and wring out gently to remove surplus water. Spread a large polythene sheet on a flat surface and place the wet silk on the sheet. Scrunch and crumple the silk at regular intervals with your hands, Mop up any pools of water from the polythene using kitchen towels.

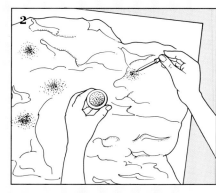

2 Apply splodges of paint randomly across the scrunched fabric using a separate eye dropper for each colour. Begin with yellow, then add green and turquoise. Allow the colours to blend and mingle on the wet fabric, but leave spaces between the splodges so that some of the white fabric remains uncoloured. Allow the fabric to dry completely before lifting it off the polythene. Fix the paint following step 6 on page 14, or according to the manufacturer's instructions. Turn a narrow hem round the fabric and machine stitch using matching thread.

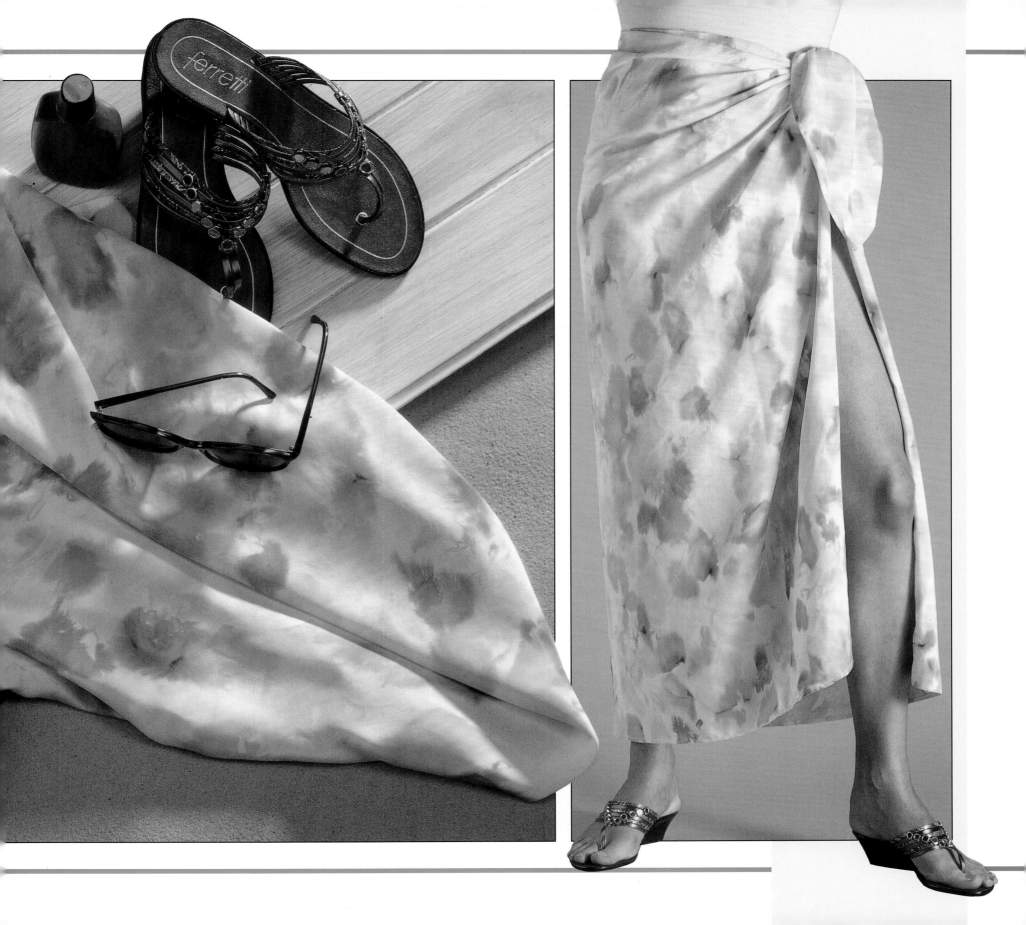

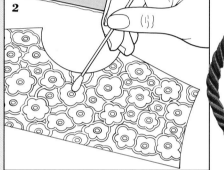

1 Press the fabric. Cut out the paper pattern pieces. Lay the front yoke pattern piece on the Habotai silk and draw round the edge with the embroidery marker so you have the complete front shape marked out. Cut out a rectangle of silk containing the yoke outline plus a margin about 5cm (2in) all round. Pin to the frame with 3-point pins.

2 Trace off the flower template on page 103 and following the Transferring technique on page 20 transfer the design to the yoke. Following the Silk Painting technique on page 14-15, outline the outside edge of the yoke and the flower pattern with clear outliner. Allow to dry, colour in the design with cotton buds. Allow to dry, then fix the paints. Make up the garment using matching sewing thread.

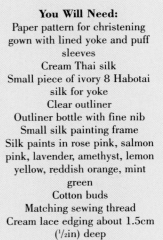

▲ *The front yoke is patterned with tiny flower heads painted in delicate pastel shades. If you prefer use different colourways.*

◀ *Make this Thai silk christening gown for someone special. Or buy a ready-made christening gown and paint it.*

You Will Need:
Paper pattern for christening gown with lined yoke and puff sleeves
Cream Thai silk
Small piece of ivory 8 Habotai silk for yoke
Clear outliner
Outliner bottle with fine nib
Small silk painting frame
Silk paints in rose pink, salmon pink, lavender, amethyst, lemon yellow, reddish orange, mint green
Cotton buds
Matching sewing thread
Cream lace edging about 1.5cm (¹/₂in) deep
Fade-away embroidery marker

Stepping Out

You Will Need:
Paper pattern for lined waistcoat
without darts
Cream 8 Habotai silk
Terracotta 8 Habotai silk for back
panel and lining
Silver outliner
Outliner bottle with fine nib
Large silk painting frame
Silk paints in silver grey, rust,
onyx
Cotton buds
Lightweight iron-on interfacing
Matching sewing thread
Fade-away embroidery marker

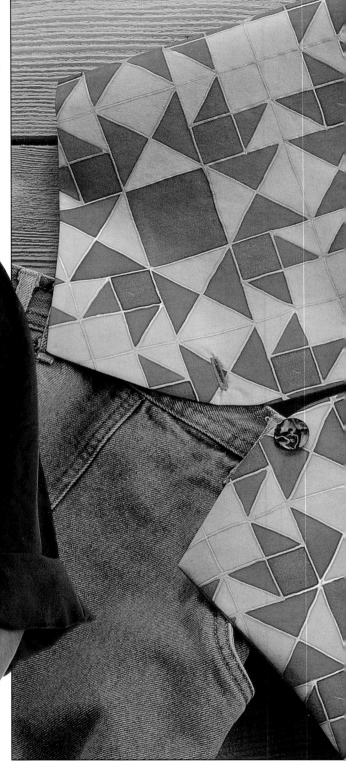

▶ *Patterned with a
traditional patchwork
of block motifs painted
in subtle shades of grey
and terracotta, this
waistcoat looks good on
both men and women.*

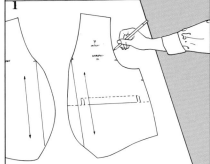

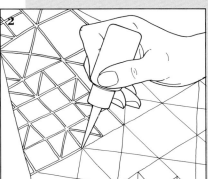

1 *Press the cream silk. Cut out the paper pattern pieces. Lay the front pattern piece on the silk and draw round it with the embroidery marker, then turn it over and position it about 5cm (2in) away from the first piece before drawing round it again. You now have one left and one right front. Cut out a rectangle of silk containing both the front outlines plus a margin of 5cm (2in) round the edge and pin to the frame with 3-point pins.*

2 *Trace off the waistcoat template on page 103 and transfer the design to the front pieces with the embroidery marker, making sure that the patterns line up. Following the Silk Painting technique on page 14-15, outline with silver outliner and colour in the pattern with cotton buds. Allow to dry, then fix the paint. Back the painted silk with interfacing following the technique on page 20, and make up the garment using matching sewing thread.*

Home Comforts

Bring a new dimension to your home furnishings with a touch of silk. Make an amazing wallhanging for the living or dining room, add soft touches to the sofa with pretty painted cushions, or enhance a bedside table with seaside mementoes.

▲ *Use the close-up photograph as a colour guide, or alter the colour scheme to co-ordinate with your home.*

▶ *Make a pretty overcloth for a circular occasional table by painting a stylish floral motif in each corner of a large ready-made square scarf.*

1 *Trace off the overcloth template given on page 103. Transfer the design to each corner of the scarf using the embroidery marker, positioning each tracing about 10cm (4in) in from the edge. Pin the scarf to the frame using map tacks inserted through the hem. Following the Silk Painting technique on page 14-15, outline the designs with pink outliner and allow to dry thoroughly.*

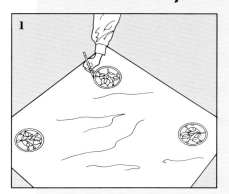

2 *Colour in each design using one colour of paint and working from the centre outwards to avoid smudging. Allow this colour to dry, then fill in the remaining colours one by one, allowing each colour to dry before proceeding to the next. Fix the paints, then place the tablecloth over a round table covered with a plain undercloth in a toning colour.*

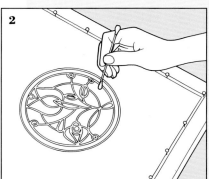

You Will Need:
90cm (36in) square ivory 8
Habotai silk scarf
Pink outliner
Outliner bottle with fine nib
Silk paints in sand, mint green, maytime green, lavender, rose pink, salmon pink
Large silk painting frame
Map tacks
Paintbrushes or cotton buds
Fade-away embroidery marker

1 *Prepare the fabric by immersing it in a salt solution following the technique given on page 16. Use a slightly stronger solution than usual, about 5 tablespoons of cooking salt to every half litre of water, and leave the fabric to soak for about ten minutes. Remove the fabric and hang up to drip dry.*

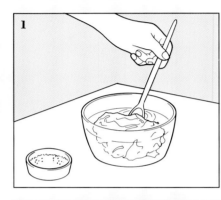

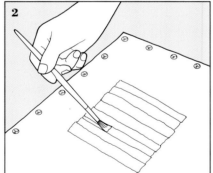

2 *Pin the fabric in the frame using 3-point silk pins. Using a large brush, paint horizontal lines of colour across the fabric, working downwards from the top of the frame. Begin by colouring the sky, painting wide, overlapping stripes of ice blue and opal blue.*

You Will Need:
50cm (20in) square white 8
Habotai silk
Silk painting frame
3-point silk pins
Salt solution
Silk paints in ice blue, opal blue, turquoise, pastel yellow, old gold
Large paintbrush
Fade-away embroidery marker
Black textile marker with fine point
Iron-on pelmet interfacing
Two matching picture frames with 10 x 15cm (4 x 6in) apertures

▶ *Salt-treated fabric can be used to make wonderful pictures. A seascape design has been created here, but a sunset would also work well.*

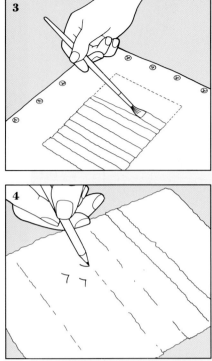

3 *Before the sky dries, paint a narrow stripe of turquoise just below it to make the sea. Allow the paint to dry. For the sand paint wide stripes of pastel yellow below the sea. Quickly, before the pastel yellow dries, add a wide stripe of old gold where the sand meets the sea. Allow to dry, then fix the paint colours.*

4 *Take the backing and glass out of the frames. Place both frames on the painted silk, one vertically and one horizontally, and move them around until you have a pleasing picture showing. Try to have more sky in the vertical frame and more sand in the horizontal frame. Mark the positions with the embroidery marker, remove the frames and cut out, leaving a 2.5cm (1in) margin all round. Back with interfacing following the technique on page 20. Using the textile marker, draw two or three 'V' shapes in the sky of the vertical picture to represent seagulls, then mount the pictures.*

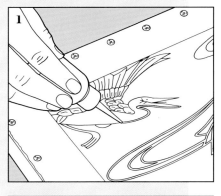

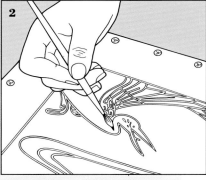

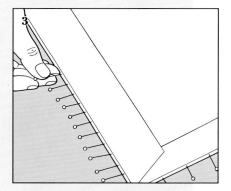

1 *Trace off the wallhanging template given on page 103, enlarge it to the correct size and transfer the design to the fabric. Following the Silk Painting technique on page 14-15, outline the cranes and blue stripes with silver outliner. Work from the centre of the design outwards, and also outline the square containing the whole design. Allow to dry, then outline the crane symbol at the lower left hand corner of the design with gold outliner.*

2 *Using the photograph as a guide, colour in the design using one colour of paint and again working from the centre outwards. Allow this colour to dry, then fill in the remaining colours one by one, allowing each colour to dry before proceeding to the next. Finally, colour in about 5cm (2in) of fabric outside the square outline using Prussian blue. Fix the colours, then back the painted silk with interfacing following the technique given on page 20.*

3 *Apply fabric glue evenly to one side of the card, place the wadding over the top, press gently in place and allow to dry. Centring the design, lay the painted fabric face up over the wadding-covered card and trim away some of the surplus fabric round the edge, so the silk is about 5cm (2in) larger than the card. Keeping the design centralised, fold the top fabric edge over the card and push glass-headed pins in along this side of the picture, going through the fabric and right into the edge of the card. Repeat along the lower edge, pulling the two sides, folding into the corner neatly.*

▶ *Stylized Japanese cranes and flowing streams of water make a stunning wall decoration. Take inspiration from Japanese or Chinese paintings if you want to create a different design.*

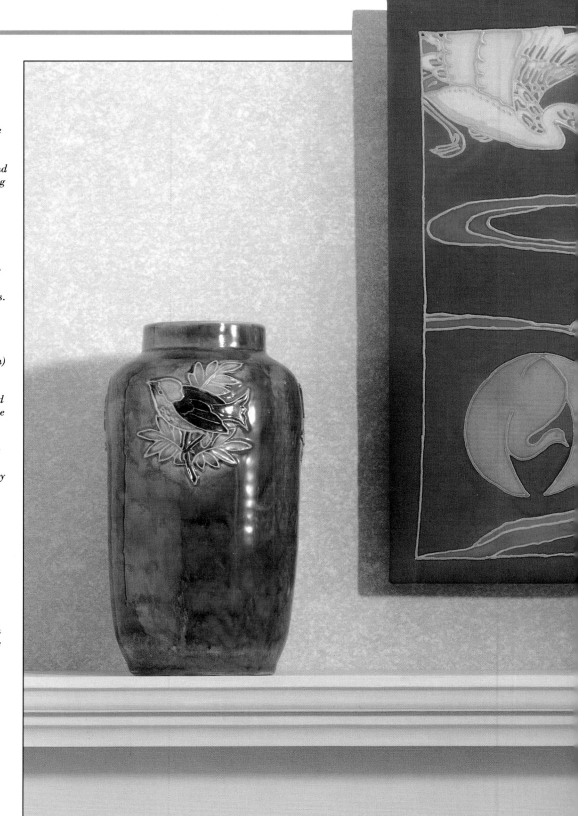

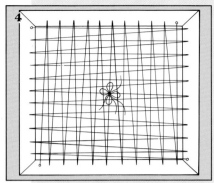

4 *Turn the picture over. Thread the needle with string or crochet cotton, make a firm knot at the end, then lace the string alternately from top to bottom until you reach the centre of the picture. If you run out of string before you reach the centre, join another length to the first one with a reef knot. Repeat the lacing in the other direction, then pull the string to tighten the fabric evenly and tie in a bow at the centre. Repeat this procedure along the remaining two sides. Stitch a small brass ring close to each of the top corners for hanging the picture.*

You Will Need:
50cm (20in) square white 8
Habotai silk
Large silk painting frame
3-point silk pins
Gold and silver outliner
Outliner bottle with fine nib
Silk paints in silver grey, blue
grey, salmon pink, orange, azure
blue, Prussian blue
Paintbrushes
Lightweight iron-on interfacing
36cm (14in) square thick card
36cm (14in) square lightweight
polyester wadding
Fabric glue
Glass-headed pins
Fine string or crochet cotton
Large crewel needle
Two small brass rings
Sewing thread and needle

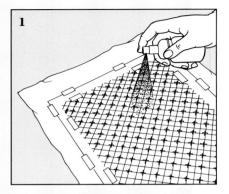

1 For the napkin rings, spread out the polythene on a flat surface, place the silk on it and tape to secure. Lay the lace over the fabric and secure again. Transfer the lightest paint colour to the atomiser bottle and spray the lace at random. Repeat with the other colours, until the background is covered. Allow to dry, then fix the colour.

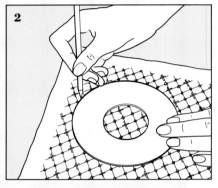

2 Back the silk with interfacing following the technique on page 20. Cut into 15cm (¹/₂in) squares and bond two squares together, with wrong sides facing. Repeat, until you have a bonded square for each napkin ring. Transfer the doughnut-shaped template on page 103 on to the card, and cut out with a craft knife. Place the template on a bonded square and draw round it. Machine satin stitch around the inner circle and trim the centre of the ring. Finally, trim the fabric round the outer circle with pinking scissors.

The napkin rings are patterned with a sprayed, lace-effect using a range of soft blues and greens.

▶ *Decorate a small, square scarf and weight the corners with beads to make a pretty lampshade cover.*

You Will Need:
NAPKIN RING:
Pale pink silk taffeta
Polyester lace with a small pattern
Silk paints in sap green, maytime green, emerald green, turquoise, ultramarine blue
Paint diffuser or atomiser bottle
Eye dropper, Polythene sheet and Masking tape
Iron-on pelmet interfacing
Fusible bonding web
Sewing thread to tone
Pinking scissors, Thin card and Craft knife
Fade-away embroidery marker

You Will Need:
HANDKERCHIEF LAMPSHADE:
55cm (22in) square turquoise 8 Habotai silk scarf
Silk painting frame, Map tacks and Gold outliner
Outliner bottle with fine nib
Silk paints in primrose yellow, reddish orange, raspberry, oriental green, turquoise, bright blue, blue grey
Paintbrushes or cotton buds
Matching sewing thread
Four long brass beads with vertical holes
Four small round brass beads
Sewing needle

1 *The lampshade design is drawn freehand and then outlined directly on to the fabric. Following the Silk Painting technique on page 14-15, pin the silk to the frame and outline the design with gold outliner, working from the centre outwards to avoid smudging. Allow the outliner to dry. Colour in the design using one colour of paint. Allow to dry, then fill in the remaining colours one by one, allowing each colour to dry before proceeding to the next. Fix the paint.*

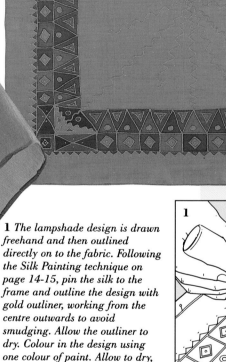

2 *Using matching sewing thread, sew one long and one round bead to each corner. Secure the thread at the corner, take the needle down the long bead, through the round bead and then back through the long bead. Gently tighten the thread so the beads sit close to the corner, then secure the thread end neatly on the wrong side. Drape the silk square over a small white coolie lampshade.*

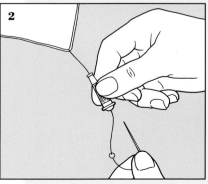

75

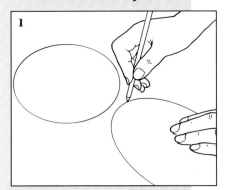

1 *Paint several pictures at the same time on a large piece of silk. Remove the glass or acetate circles from the frames and position them on the silk about 5cm (2in) apart. Carefully draw round each circle and oval with the embroidery marker. Trace off the templates given on page 104, and transfer one motif to the centre of each outlined shape.*

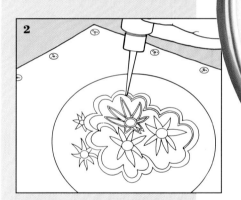

2 *Pin the fabric to the frame using 3-point silk pins. Following the Silk Painting technique on page 14-15, outline the designs with silver or lilac outliner, working outwards from the centre of the fabric to avoid smudging. Allow the outliner to dry for several hours.*

▶ *A small hand-painted picture would make a wonderful gift for someone special. Here floral designs offer inspiration, but the theme could be animals.*

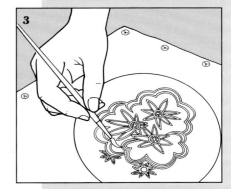

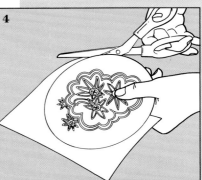

You Will Need:
White 8 Habotai silk
Silk painting frame
Outliner bottle with fine nib
Paintbrushes
Iron-on pelmet interfacing
Fade-away embroidery marker

TULIP PICTURE:
Silver outliner
Silk paints in amethyst, rose
pink, cyclamen pink, reddish
orange, yellowish green, olive
green
Circular wooden frame with 8cm
(3in) aperture

CHRYSANTHEMUM PICTURE:
Lilac outliner
Silk paints in amethyst, ice blue,
orange, pistachio green, olive
green, rose pink, cyclamen,
Bordeaux pink
Circular wooden frame with 10cm
(4in) aperture

BOUQUET WITH BOW:
Silver outliner
Silk paints in amethyst, rose
pink, cyclamen pink, reddish
orange, yellowish green, olive
green
Oval brass frame with 12 x 17cm
(4³⁄₄ x 6³⁄₄in) aperture

TINY FLOWERS:
Lilac outliner
Silk paints in mint green, grass
green, pistachio green, azure
blue, rose pink, carmine red
Circular brass frame with 15cm
(6in) aperture

PINK FLOWERS:
Lilac outliner
Silk paints in grass green,
yellowish green, olive green,
salmon pink, flesh pink,
mandarin yellow, reddish orange
Circular brass frame with 15cm
(6in) aperture

3 *Colour in the flower motifs with
a paintbrush, using the
photograph as a colour guide.
Complete all the areas worked in
one colour first and allow to dry.
Fill in the remaining colours one
by one, allowing the paint to dry
between applications. When the
painted silk is completely dry,
remove the silk from the frame,
then fix the colours following step
6 on page 14, or according to the
manufacturer's instructions.*

4 *Cut out the circles or ovals,
allowing a margin about 2.5cm
(1in) all round. Back the pieces of
painted silk with interfacing
following the technique on page
20, then cut out each design
along the circular or oval outline.
Following the manufacturer's
instructions, mount the silk pieces
in the frames.*

Home Comforts

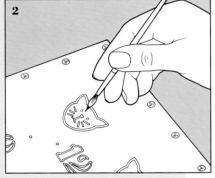

1 *Trace off the clock face template given on page 105, and transfer it to the silk. Pin the silk to the frame with 3-point silk pins. Following the Silk Painting technique on page 14-15, outline the design with copper outliner. Work from the centre of the design outwards to avoid smudging. Allow to dry thoroughly.*

2 *Using the photograph as a guide, colour in the design with a paintbrush. Apply each colour separately, and allow to dry thoroughly between each colour. Back the painted silk with iron-on pelmet interfacing following the instructions given on page 20. Following the manufacturer's instructions, mount the painted silk in the clock.*

You Will Need:
CAT CLOCK:
25cm (10in) x 30cm (12in) ivory 8 Habotai silk
Copper outliner and an Outliner bottle with fine nib
Silk paints in russet brown, blue grey, turquoise
Silk painting frame, 3-point silk pins and Paintbrushes
Wooden clock from Framecraft
(Details on page 108.)
Iron-on pelmet interfacing

You Will Need:
WRAPPED VASE:
Piece of yellow 8 Habotai silk large enough to cover the vase,
plus about 10cm (4in) extra all round
Clear outliner and an Outliner bottle with fine nib
Silk paints in dark grey, orange, salmon pink
Silk painting frame, 3-point silk pins, Paintbrushes or cotton buds and Eye droppers
Vase about 18cm (7in) high with neck, Length of 1.5cm ($\frac{1}{2}$in) wide braid to tone
Large rubber band, PVA craft medium, Old paintbrush and an Old saucer

◀ ▶ *Four happy cats decorate a wooden mantle clock, making a perfect gift for any cat lover. Wrapping a vase is a great way to hide any ugly or chipped pie*

1 Pin the fabric in the frame using 3-point pins. Following the technique for Silk Painting on page 14-15, draw spirals of clear outliner at random across the silk, making sure that the end of each spiral is closed with outliner. Allow to dry, then paint the spirals dark grey. Using the eye droppers, drop spots of orange and salmon pink on to the yellow background. Allow to dry, then fix the paint.

2 Pour some PVA into the saucer and dilute with cold water to the consistency of thin cream. Stand the vase at the centre of the silk, pull the fabric up to the top of the vase and secure with a rubber band. Cut away the surplus, leaving about 2.5cm (1in) protruding at the top of the vase. Using the old paintbrush, saturate the fabric at both sides of the rubber band with PVA. Press the surplus fabric inside the vase, and add more PVA to stick it in place. Stick the braid round the neck, and leave to dry.

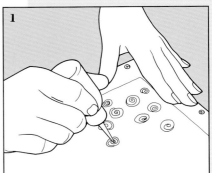

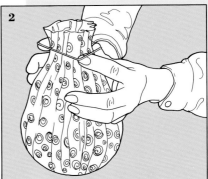

1 *All three designs are drawn freehand and outlined directly on to the fabric. Use the close-up photographs as a guide. Following the Silk Painting technique on page 14-15, pin the silk to the frame and draw on the design with clear outliner, working from the centre outwards to avoid smudging. Allow outliner to dry.*

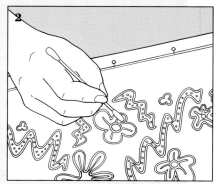

2 *Colour in the design using one colour of paint and work from the centre outwards. Allow this colour to dry, then fill in the remaining colours one by one, allowing each colour to dry, before proceeding to the next. Fix the paints. Cut out each design leaving a margin of about 1.5cm (¹/₂in) around the edge. Back each piece of painted silk with iron-on interfacing and make up the cushion cover. Insert the cushion pad and slipstich the opening closed.*

SQUARE GEOMETRIC CUSHION:
45cm (18in) square white 8
Habotai silk
Silk paints in mint green,
pistachio green, violet, purple,
yellow, maroon, pale blue,
turquoise, petrol blue,
ultramarine
40cm (16in) square cushion pad

RECTANGULAR FLORAL CUSHION:
35 x 45cm (14 x 18in) white 8
Habotai silk
Silk paints in mint green, grass
green, pistachio green, violet,
purple, yellow, rose pink,
cyclamen pink, Bordeaux pink,
pale blue, turquoise, petrol blue,
ultramarine
30 x 38cm (12 x 15in)
cushion pad

SQUARE FLORAL CUSHION:
40cm (16in) square white 8
Habotai silk
Silk paints in mint green, grass
green, purple, yellow, reddish
orange, rose pink, cyclamen pink,
Bordeaux pink
35cm (14in) square cushion pad

◀ *Make a group of
co-ordinating cushion covers by
varying the patterns, but keeping
the colours the same.*

You Will Need:
Clear outliner
Outliner bottle with fine nib
Silk painting frame
3-point silk pins
Paintbrushes or cotton buds
Fade-away embroidery marker
Lightweight iron-on interfacing
Backing fabric and sewing
threads to tone

Perfect Presents

The texture and feel of silk makes it a wonderful fabric
to make into special gifts for family and friends.
Personalise your hand-painted presents
by using different colours, or creating
new designs suitable for the recipient.
Then, make silk-painted cards to add
extra extravagance to the occasion.

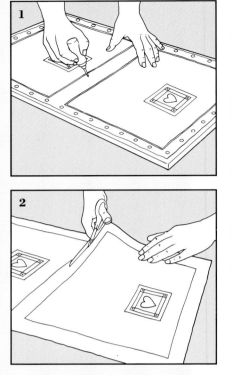

1 Paint several bags at once. Draw the outline of the bags to the desired size on a piece of white silk, allowing about 8cm (3in) between each bag. Trace off the heart templates given on page 104-105, and transfer to each bag. Stretch the fabric in the frame. Outline the designs and the outside edge of each bag with silver outliner, following the technique on page 14. Leave the outliner to dry.

2 Following the Silk Painting technique on page 14-15, fill in the heart designs and backgrounds with silk paints, using the photograph as a colour guide. Allow the paint to dry for several hours, remove the silk from the frame, then fix the paints following step 6, on page 14, or according to the manufacturer's instructions. Cut out each design leaving a margin of about 1.5cm (¹/₂in) around each one.

3 *Back each piece of painted silk with iron-on interfacing. Fold in half and machine stitch along the side to make a seam. Press the seam open. Fold the bag so the seam falls along the centre back, then machine along the lower edge and press the seam. Clip off surplus fabric at the lower corners, then turn the bag to the right side and press. Trim the top of the bag with pinking scissors to make a decorative edge. Wrap the gift in tissue paper and place in the bag. Tie the top of the bag with silver cord or ribbon.*

1 *To make the herb pillow, trace off the rose template given on page 105, and transfer to one square of white fabric. Following the Silk Painting technique on page 14-15, outline and colour in with silk paints, then colour the second silk square with bright blue paint to make the pillow back. Back each piece of silk with interfacing and make up the pillow following the Making a Cushion Cover technique on page 21. Stuff the pillow loosely with a mixture of polyester stuffing and rose petals and slipstitch the opening closed. Finally, tie a short length of silver cord into a bow at each corner of the pillow.*

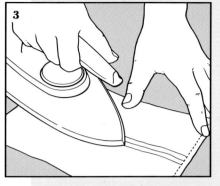

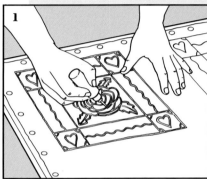

You Will Need:
HERB PILLOW:
Two 23cm (9in) squares of white
8 Habotai silk
Silver outliner
Outliner bottle with fine nib
Silk paints in bright blue,
turquoise, turquoise green, pale
pink, cyclamen pink, Bordeaux
red, violet, ice blue, pistachio
green, olive green
Silk painting frame
3-point silk pins
Paintbrushes and cotton buds
Lightweight iron-on interfacing
Sewing thread to tone
Narrow silver cord
White polyester toy stuffing
Dried rose petals or other
strongly-scented pot pourri

▲ *Keep your clothes smelling sweet with this lovely scented pillow. It's ideal for the bottom drawer.*

◄ *Filled with pot pourri or sugared almonds, these pretty gift bags will make a perfect present for special friends.*

You Will Need:
GIFT BAGS:
White 8 Habotai silk
Silver outliner
Outliner bottle with fine nib
Silk paints in bright blue,
turquoise, turquoise green, pale
pink, cyclamen pink, Bordeaux
red, violet
Silk painting frame
3-point silk pins
Paintbrushes or cotton buds
Lightweight iron-on interfacing
Sewing threads to tone
Silver cord or ribbon
Pinking scissors

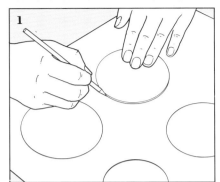

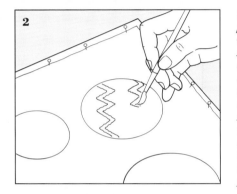

1 *Prepare the fabric by immersing it in salt solution following the technique given on page 16, and leave it to dry. Paint several box lids at the same time. Remove the acetate circles from the box lids, lay them on the silk about 5cm (2in) apart and draw round them with a pencil. Pin the fabric in the frame.*

2 *Paint the zigzag designs with a paintbrush. Load a medium brush with colour, then quickly paint a zigzag line across the drawn circle, extending the line at each end about 1.5cm (½in) beyond the circle. Using the photograph as a colour guide, paint several zigzag lines, arranging them in regular stripes or altering the slope to create diamond shapes between the lines. Finally, add the tiny dots and lines with a fine paintbrush.*

You Will Need:
Small pieces of ivory 8
Habotai silk
Salt solution
Silk painting frame
3-point silk pins
Iron-on pelmet interfacing

ZIGZAG BOXES:
Silk paints in ochre, old gold, bronze, mandarin yellow, orange, carmine red, rust brown, chestnut brown, dark brown, black
Paintbrushes
Mahogany finish trinket boxes from Framecraft (Details on page 108.)

SPOTTED BOXES:
Silk paints in pastel yellow, sand, ochre, bronze, carmine red, rust brown, chestnut brown, dark brown, black
Cotton buds
Elm finish trinket boxes from Framecraft (Details on page 108.)

▶ *The lids of these wooden boxes are painted with African patterns on salt treated fabrics.*

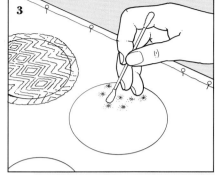

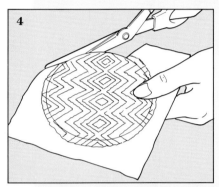

3 *For the spotted designs, make a pattern of large spots inside each circular outline using a cotton bud. Use either pastel yellow, sand or ochre paint and allow the spots to dry for two or three minutes. Add further spots of colour to the centre or the base of these spots, building up the colours from light to dark. Allow the paint to dry slightly between each application.*

4 *Allow the paint to dry for several hours, remove the silk from the frame and fix the paints. Back the painted silk with interfacing following the technique given on page 20, then cut out each design along the circular outline. Following the manufacturer's instructions, mount the silk in the box lids.*

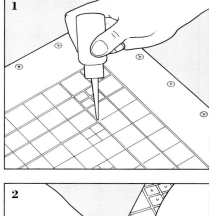

1 *Paint several bookmarks at once on a piece of silk, allowing an area of 8 x 20cm (3 x 8in) of painted silk for each bookmark. Pin the fabric to the frame with 3-point pins. Following the Silk Painting technique on page 14-15, outline the designs freehand on the silk with gold outliner, using the photographs as a guide, then colour in. Leave to dry, then fix the paint.*

2 *Using spray adhesive, stick the painted silk to the card. Trace off the template on page 104, transfer to a piece of spare card and cut out. Place the template over the silk, draw round it and cut out. Make a small hole with the point of a pair of scissors about 1.5cm (¹/₂in) from the pointed end of the bookmark. Open the arms of a paper fastener, insert the tassel loop and then close the arms. Insert the arms through the hole so the tassel lies neatly on the right side of the bookmark, and secure the fastener.*

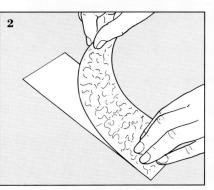

You Will Need:
BOOKMARKS WITH TASSELS:
White 8 Habotai silk
Gold outliner
Outliner bottle with fine nib
Silk paints in turquoise, grass green, jade green, pistachio green, ultramarine
Silk painting frame
3-point silk pins
Paintbrushes or cotton buds
Brass paper fasteners
Ready-made gold tassels about 10cm (4in) long (including loop)
Thin white card
Spray adhesive
Craft knife and cutting mat

You Will Need:
MARBLED BOOKMARKS:
Small strips white 8 Habotai silk
Effect salt and sea salt
Silk paints in rose pink, lavender, azure blue, ultramarine blue, grass green, opal, turquoise
Cotton buds
Eye droppers
Polythene sheet
Thin white card
Spray adhesive
Craft knife and cutting mat

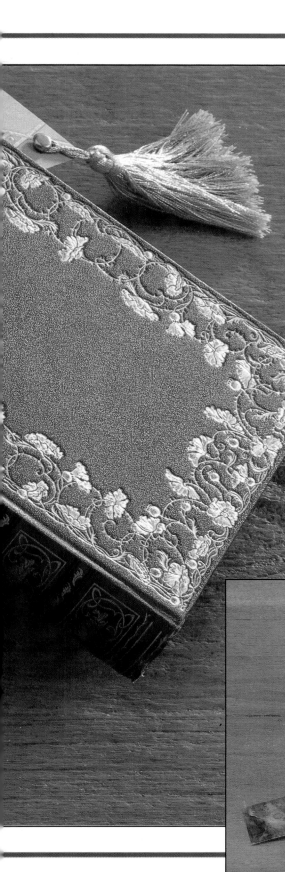

◀ ▼ *Make a special gift for a bookworm, with a selection of silk bookmarks. All the bookmarks here have been made by cutting the fabric on an angle, but you could simply make checked, or striped bookmarks.*

1 *To make the marbled bookmarks, lay the polythene sheet on a flat surface and place the silk on top. Use a separate eye dropper for each colour, drop spots of colour on to the dry silk. Spray lightly with water so the colours blend. Then sprinkle with effect salt and leave to dry.*

2 *Brush off the salt grains and fix the colours following step 6, on page 14, or according to the manufacturer's instructions. Wash the painted silk in cold water to remove the salt grains and leave to dry. Using spray adhesive, stick the fabric strips on to the card. Cut out a 5 x 20cm (2 x 8in) strip for each bookmark.*

89

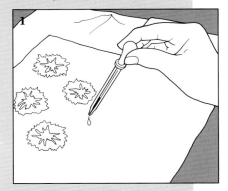

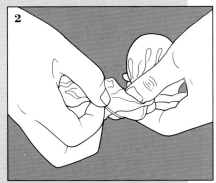

You Will Need:
LAVENDER BAGS:
White Habotai or spun silk
handkerchiefs
White 5 Habotai silk
Silk paints in ice blue, lavender,
violet, rose pink, amethyst
Eye droppers and Polythene sheet
Pinking scissors
Elastic bands
1.5cm (½in) wide sheer ribbon
to tone
Dried lavender flowers or
strongly-scented pot pourri

1 *For the lavender bags lay the polythene sheet on a flat surface and place the handkerchiefs on top. For the palest bag, spray the fabric lightly with water, then drop spots of ice blue, lavender and amethyst on top and leave to blend. For the spotted bag, drop spots of violet on the fabric and allow to dry for 2-3 minutes. Spray with water, then the same colours as before. When almost dry drop on spots of rose pink. For the small bag, drop spots of rose pink, lavender, amethyst and violet on to dry fabric and allow the colours to blend.*

2 *When the silk is completely dry, fix the colours. Using pinking scissors, cut a square of white Habotai 4cm (1½in) smaller than each scarf. Place a large spoonful of lavender in the centre of the silk, gather the silk up round the lavender and secure with an elastic band. Place in the centre of the handkerchief, gather up and secure with a length of ribbon tied in a bow.*

▶ *Make a pincushion for a friend or relative who enjoys sewing. Alternatively give a lavender bag as a special gift.*

1 *To make the pincushions, lay the polythene sheet on a flat surface, place the silk pieces on top and secure with masking tape. Position plastic alphabet stencils over the silk and secure with tape. Pour some paint into the atomiser botile and spray over one stencil. Repeat with the other two colours.*

You Will Need:

ALPHABET PINCUSHIONS:

Small pieces of silk dupion in
shades of pink, blue, turquoise
Paint diffuser or atomiser bottle
Silk paints in azure blue, dark
turquoise, cyclamen pink
Three plastic stencils with
different alphabets
Polythene sheet
Masking tape
Small piece of thin card
Sewing threads to tone
White polyester toy stuffing

2 *Carefully remove the stencils
and allow the paint to dry. Fix the
paints following step 6, on page
14, or according to the
manufacturer's instructions. Trace
off the template on page 107,
transfer to the card and cut out.
Position the template over the
painted silk and draw round the
edge. This line is the stitching
line. Make up the pincushions
following the technique on page
21, stuff firmly with toy stuffing
and slipstitch the opening closed.*

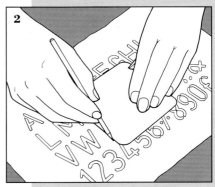

Perfect Presents

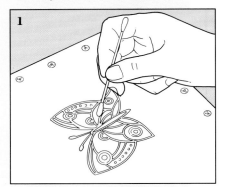

1 *Paint several butterfly designs at the same time on one piece of silk. Transfer the butterfly templates on page 106 to the silk, outline and paint. Fix the colours, then back with interfacing.*

You Will Need:
White 8 Habotai silk
Silver outliner
Outliner bottle with fine nib
Silk painting frame
3-point silk pins
Paintbrushes or cotton buds
Lightweight iron-on interfacing
Face-away embroidery marker

BUTTERFLY CARDS:
Silk paints in primary yellow,
mandarin yellow, orange, light
vermilion red, raspberry pink,
purple, bright blue, Parisian blue,
oriental green, emerald green,
dark turquoise
Silver card
Spray adhesive
Pinking scissors

CHRISTMAS CARDS:
Effect salt
Silk paints in carmine red,
oriental green, pine green, bright
blue, purple, mandarin yellow,
dark ochre, dark brown
White opaque fabric paint
Ready-cut white greeting cards
with 9.5cm (3³/₄in) circular,
8 x 10cm (3 x 4in) oval,
7 x 11cm (2³/₄ x 4¹/₄in)
rectangular apertures
Double-sided sticky tape

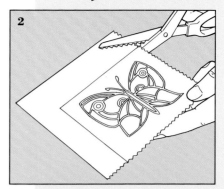

2 *Using pinking scissors, cut each butterfly design into a rectangular shape, allowing a margin of about 1.5cm (¹/₂in) round the edge. Cut the silver card into rectangles which, when folded in half, are slightly larger than the pinked silk. Using spray adhesive, stick the painted silk to one half of the card. Score and fold the card in half.*

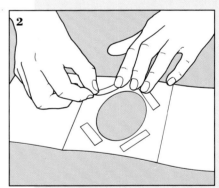

1 *For the Christmas cards, paint several cards at once on a large piece of silk. Trace off the templates given on page 106, and transfer to the silk using the embroidery marker. Pin the fabric in the frame with 3-point pins. Following the Silk Painting technique on page 14-15, outline the designs with silver outliner. Add a rectangle of outliner round each design to prevent the background colour from spreading. Colour in the designs using a paintbrush, and allow to dry. For the tree and snowman designs, colour in the designs, allow to dry, then add the background colours and sprinkle with salt while still wet. Finally, add highlights to snowman and icing with white fabric paint. Fix colours, back with interfacing.*

◀ *Perfect for Christmas, this range of painted cards are mounted in ready-cut greeting cards to give a professional finish.*

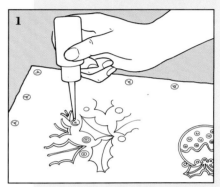

2 *Centre the design over the aperture in the card and trim away the surplus fabric, allowing a margin of about 1.5cm (¹/₂in) to overlap the aperture. Place the design right side up on a flat surface. On the wrong side of the card, stick strips of double-sided tape around the aperture. Peel off the backing, then position the aperture over the painted design and press in place. Again using tape, stick the flap down over the back of the silk.*

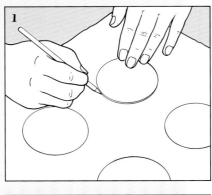

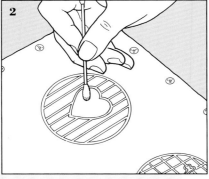

1 *Paint several box lids at the same time. Remove the acetate circles from the box lids, lay them on the silk about 5cm (2in) apart and draw round them with a pencil. Trace off the heart, flower and goose templates given on page 106, and transfer to the centre of each circle. Stretch the fabric in a frame. Following the Silk Painting technique on page 14-15, outline the motifs and the outside edge of each circle with copper outliner. Allow to dry.*

2 *Fill in the motifs and backgrounds with silk paints, using the photograph as a colour guide. Allow the paint to dry, remove the silk from the frame, then fix the colours. Back the painted silk with interfacing following the technique given on page 20, then cut out each design along the circular outline. Following the manufacturer's instructions, mount the silk in the box lids.*

You Will Need:
Small pieces white 8
Habotai silk
Copper outliner
Outliner bottle with fine nib
Silk paints in carmine red,
raspberry pink, mandarin yellow,
oriental green, bright blue
Silk painting frame
3-point silk pins
Paint brushes or cotton buds
Iron-on pelmet interfacing
Silver jewellery boxes from
Framecraft (Details on page 108.)

▶ *Featuring folk art motifs, these silver plated boxes can be used to keep jewellery or mementoes safe.*

Perfect Presents

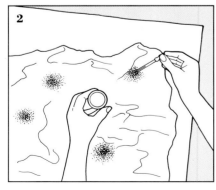

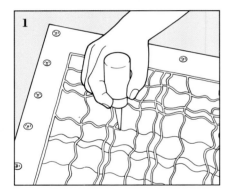

1 *To make the large notebooks, paint two or three covers at the same time on one piece of silk. Draw the outline of the covers on a large piece of white silk, allowing about 8cm (3in) between each cover. Stretch the fabric in a frame. Working freehand, outline geometric designs and the outside edge of each cover with silver outliner, following the technique on page 14. Allow to dry. Following the Silk Painting technique on page 14-15, fill in the designs with silk paints. Allow the paint to dry, remove the silk from the frame, then fix the paint. Cut out each design leaving a margin of about 1.5cm (¹/₂in) around each one.*

2 *For the small notebooks, lay the polythene sheet on a flat surface. Wet the two pieces of silk and place on the polythene, scrunching evenly. For the checked fabric, drop spots of pine green, Parisian blue and amethyst on to the silk using an eye dropper. While the paint is still wet, sprinkle with effect salt. For the striped fabric, drop spots of maroon, pine green, Parisian blue and grey on to the crumpled silk, letting the colours blend.*

3 *Allow all the paints to dry, then fix the colours. Each book is covered in the same way – wrap the fabric round the closed notebook and trim away the surplus, leaving a margin of 2.5cm (1in) all round. Open the fabric out flat, wrong side facing you. Hold the book upright and centre the spine on the fabric. Snip the fabric at the spine.*

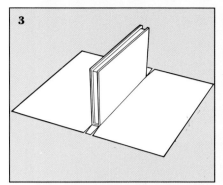

4 *Using a latex glue, dab glue sparingly at each side of the snipped fabric. Turn over the snipped edges and press them carefully in place to secure the raw edges neatly. Allow the glue to dry completely.*

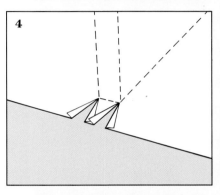

◀ *Make your notebooks individual with silk painted covers. It is one way to ensure you can find them easily.*

5 *Replace the book on the fabric. Place a tiny dab of glue on the central snipped tab of fabric and carefully push the tab into the book spine using the point of a small pair of scissors. Lay the book flat and wrap the fabric over the closed book. Lift the upper cover and pages and use a small weight such as a paperweight to hold them clear of the lower cover.*

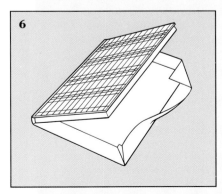

6 *Working on the lower cover first, turn the fabric over at the corners and stick in place inside the cover. Stick the remaining raw fabric edges to the inside of the cover, making sure that they lie flat. Turn the book over and repeat for the other cover. Cut two rectangles of coloured paper to fit inside the covers. Stick in place to hide the raw edges.*

Perfect Presents

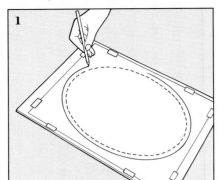

1 *Following the manufacturer's instructions, take the tray to pieces. Place the top board (with the cut-out oval) on a flat surface and centre the piece of silk on top. Secure with masking tape. Using the marker, carefully draw round the aperture 1.5cm (¹⁄₂in) from the edge to make a large oval outline on the fabric.*

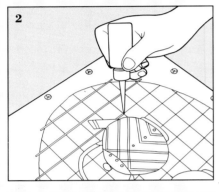

2 *Trace off the teapot template given on page 107, and transfer to the fabric using the embroidery marker, making sure that the chequerboard pattern meets the oval outline. Pin the fabric in the frame with 3-point silk pins. Outline the teapots, chequerboard background and the outside edge of the oval with clear outliner following the technique given on page 14. Allow the outliner to dry.*

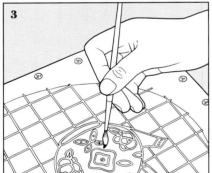

3 *Following the Silk Painting technique on page 14-15, fill in the teapot design and background with paints, using the photograph as a guide. Allow the paint to dry, remove the silk from the frame, then fix following step 6 on page 14, or according to the manufacturer's instructions. Cut out the design leaving a margin of 1.5cm (¹⁄₂in) around the edge.*

You Will Need:
40 x 55cm (16 x 22in) white 8
Habotai silk
Clear outliner
Outliner bottle with fine nib
Silk paints in carmine red, old
gold, ice blue, mid blue,
ultramarine blue
Silk painting frame, 3-point silk
pins and Paintbrushes
Rectangular wooden tray from
Framecraft (Details on page 108.)
Lightweight iron-on interfacing
Fade-away embroidery marker

▶ *Just the thing for tea for two, this charming design is cleverly mounted in a wooden tray. To keep the silk clean, the tray comes complete with a sheet of glass.*

4 Back the painted silk with iron-on interfacing following the technique given on page 20. Place the top board over the white card supplied with the tray and lightly draw round the oval with a pencil. Remove the top board. Lay the painted silk right side up over the white card, centring the design over the drawn oval. Secure in place with strips of sticky tape. Re-assemble the tray.

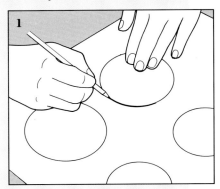

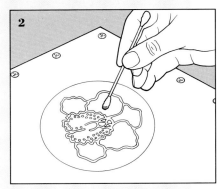

1 *Paint several bowl lids at the same time. Remove the acetate circles from the bowl lids, lay them on the silk about 5cm (2in) apart and draw round them with a pencil. Trace off the orchid templates given on page 107, and transfer the designs to the centre of each circle. Stretch the fabric in a frame with 3-point silk pins. Outline the motifs and the outside edge of each circle with clear outliner, following the technique given on page 14. Allow the outliner to dry.*

2 *Following the Silk Painting technique given on page 14-15, fill in the orchid motifs and the green background with silk paints, using the photograph as a colour guide. Allow the paint to dry, remove the silk from the frame and fix the colours. Back with interfacing, then cut out each design along the circular outline. Following the manufacturer's instructions, mount the silk in the bowl lids.*

You Will Need:
Small pieces white 8
Habotai silk
Clear outliner
Outliner bottle with fine nib
Silk painting frame
3-point silk pins
Paintbrushes or cotton buds
Cut crystal bowls with silver-plated lids from Framecraft
(Details on page 108.)
Iron-on pelmet interfacing

CYMBIDIUM ORCHID:
Silk paints in pastel yellow, mandarin yellow, ochre, mint green

PEACH ODONTOGLOSSUM ORCHID:
Silk paints in pale salmon pink, salmon pink, Bordeaux pink, plum

PINK ODONTOGLOSSUM ORCHID
Silk paints in lemon yellow, sand, rose pink, Bordeaux pink, carmine red

◀ *Luxurious hand-cut crystal bowls are decorated with the aristocrat of the flower world, the orchid.*

Templates

The following pages present the templates for the projects. Enlarge the templates on a photocopier to fit the correct size required for the piece of silk you are using.
The grid behind the templates is equal to 1cm (³/₄in) square. When working with measurements ensure you follow either metric or imperial measurements, but not a combination of both.

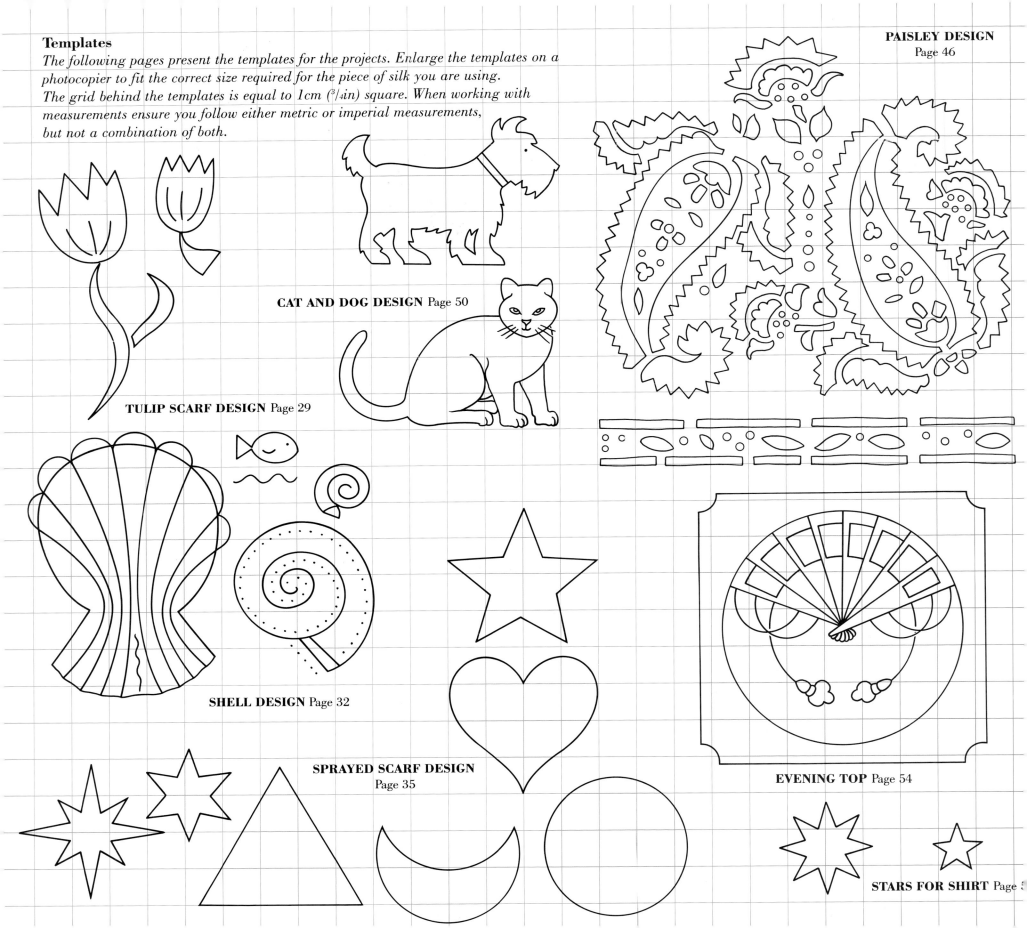

PAISLEY DESIGN
Page 46

CAT AND DOG DESIGN Page 50

TULIP SCARF DESIGN Page 29

SHELL DESIGN Page 32

SPRAYED SCARF DESIGN
Page 35

EVENING TOP Page 54

STARS FOR SHIRT Page 5

T SHIRT DESIGN Page 58

NAPKIN RING Page 74

CHRISTENING GOWN Page 62

WAISTCOAT DESIGN Page 64

TABLECLOTH DESIGN Page 68

WALLHANGING Page 72

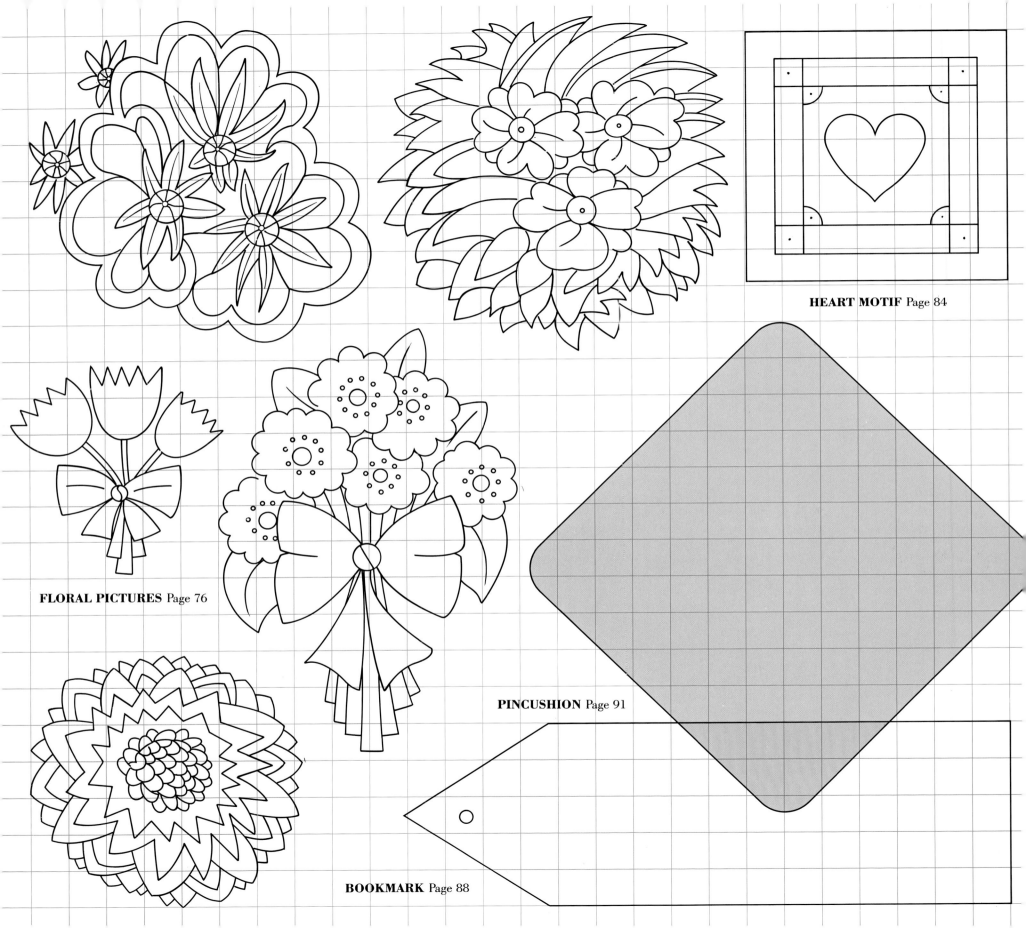

HEART MOTIF Page 84

FLORAL PICTURES Page 76

PINCUSHION Page 91

BOOKMARK Page 88

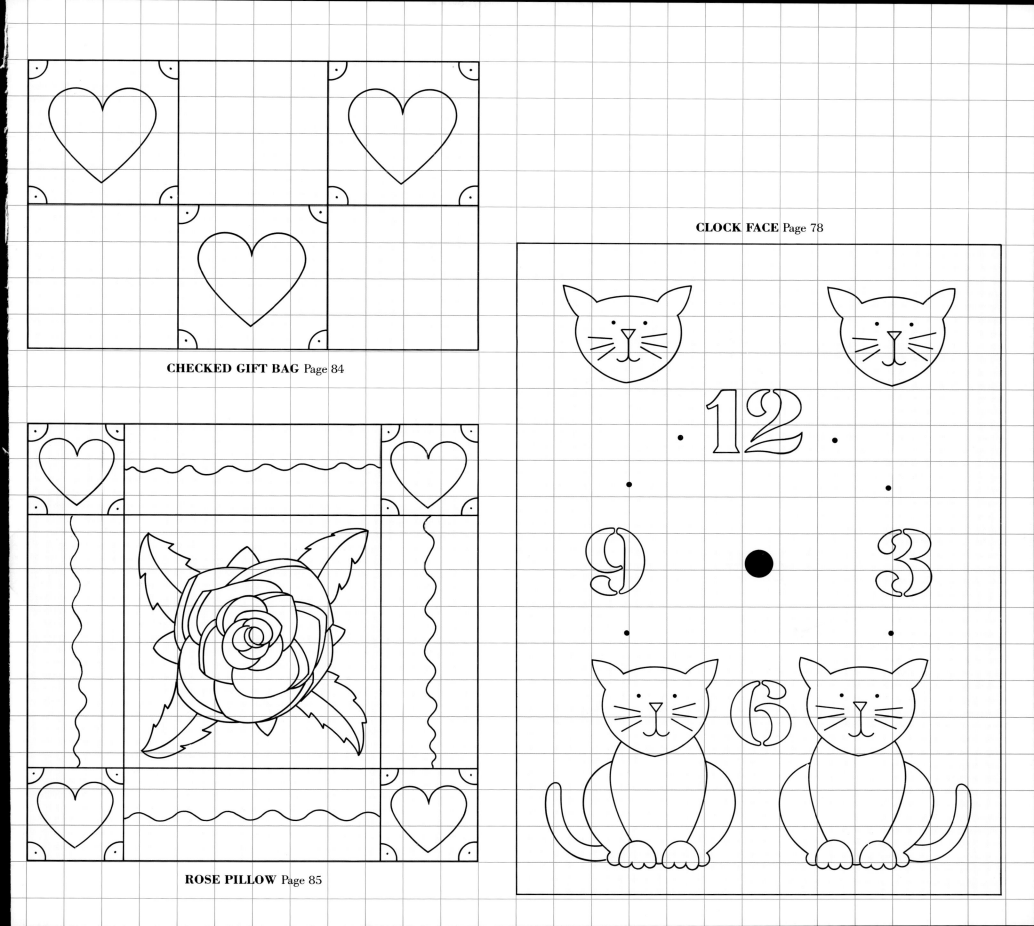

CHECKED GIFT BAG Page 84

CLOCK FACE Page 78

ROSE PILLOW Page 85

BUTTERFLY CARDS Page 92

JEWELLERY BOXES Page 94

CHRISTMAS CARDS Page 93

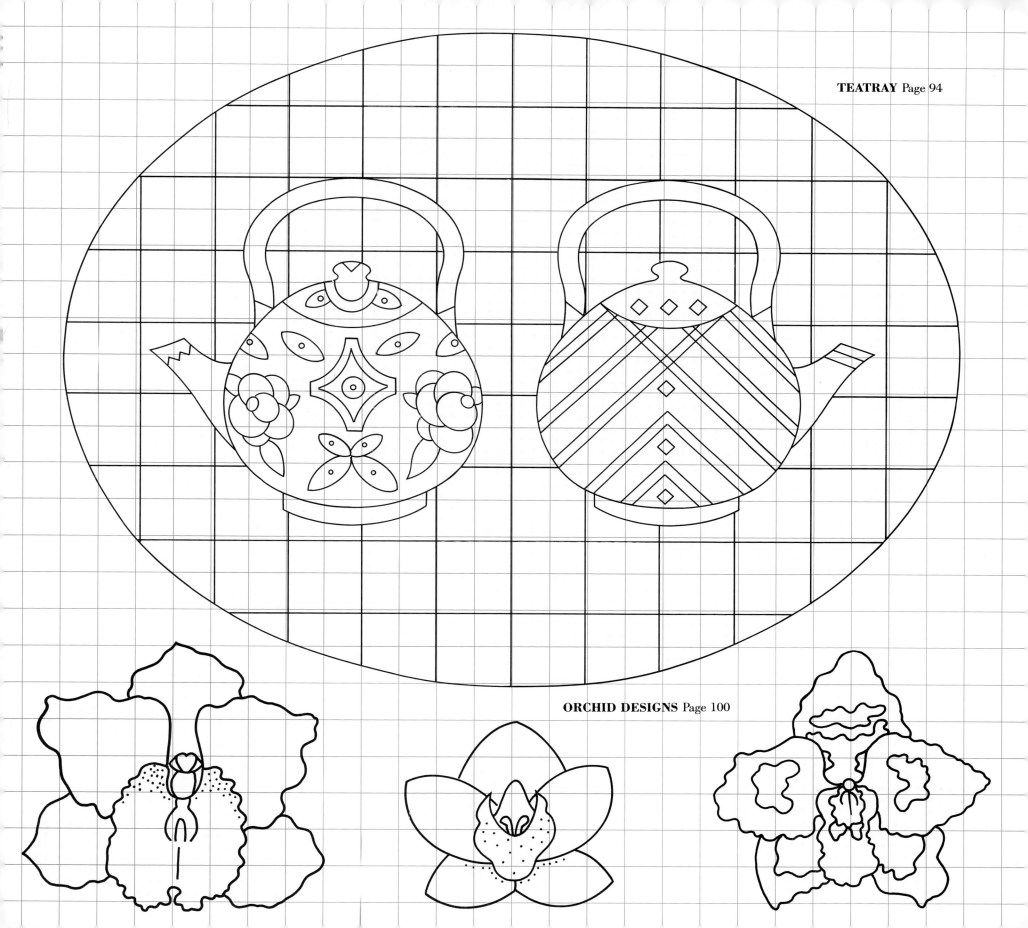

TEATRAY Page 94

ORCHID DESIGNS Page 100

Managing Editor: Jo Finnis

Editor: Sue Wilkinson

Design: Barry Savage

Photography: Steve Tanner

Illustrations: Geoff Denney Associates

Typesetting: Elaine Morris

Production: Ruth Arthur; Sally Connolly;
Neil Randles; Karen Staff; Jonathan Tickner

Production Director: Gerald Hughes

ACKNOWLEDGEMENTS

Judy Davis for making up the garments
Cheryl Owen for covering the silk painted notebooks
Pebeo, Phillip and Tacey, North Way, Andover, Hampshire, SP10 5BA for suppling the Setaskrib pens and Setasilk colours.
Paperchase, Tottenham Court Road, London, W1P 9AS. Tel 0171 580 8496 for supplying the Marabu silk paints
George Weil, 18 Hanson Street, London, W1P 7DB. Tel 0171 580 5846 for supplying silks, paints and photographic properties
Fred Aldous, PO Box 135, 37 Lever Street, Manchester 1, M60 1UX for silks and paints
Framecraft, Mail Order from Framecraft Miniatures Ltd, 372-376 Summer Lane, Hockley, Birmingham, B19 3QA. Tel 0121 212 0551